RETURN TO THE RED PLANET:
22 Days in Gorbachev's Backyard

Return to the Red Planet

22 DAYS IN GORBACHEV'S BACKYARD

MIKHAIL MORGULIS

VICTOR BOOKS ®

A DIVISION OF SCRIPTURE PRESS PUBLICATIONS INC.
USA CANADA ENGLAND

All Scripture quotations are taken from the Authorized (King James) Version.

Recommended Dewey Decimal Classification: 910.4
Suggested Subject Heading: ACCOUNT OF TRAVEL

Library of Congress Catalog Card Number: 89-60157
ISBN: 0-89693-764-X

I would like to express my thanks to:

Peter and Anita Deyneka, who advised me to write this book; Alex Leonovich, who has supplied me with the essential sustenance: love; Andrew Semenchuk, an efficient person who has done a lot for me in my life; Joel McElreath, a good American Samaritan; Platon Chartichlaa, a teacher who disclosed the light of the Bible to me; Roman Dechtiarenko, who relates to people with grace; Melanie Colón, an excellent adviser; Victor Matveiuk, for his kind heart and desire to help always; Mark Sweeney, who firmly believed that this book was important for American Christians; Maria Nasteka and Irina Platonov, who typed the drafts under difficult circumstances; that unknown herald who many years ago told me about the love of Christ; my wife Tanya, without whom I would not have written these humble notes; and all those whose prayers warmed and taught and encouraged me.

Not the mother who bore you, but
the one who raised you.
(Russian saying)

CONTENTS

PREFACE 9
INTRODUCTION 13
  1. My Return on a
     River of Memories 17
  2. Return to the Red
     Planet 25
  3. Moscow: City of
     Meetings and Mysteries.................. 33
  4. Moscow Continued:
     Missions, Mothers, and Markets 47
  5. The Gospel in Georgia 55
  6. Higher Up and Further In 61
  7. An Armenian Addendum 71
  8. A Crimean Chapter:
     Yalta and Beyond 85
  9. A Leningrad Legacy 97
  10. More Lessons in Leningrad 109
  11. Kiev: Return to My Home.................. 117
  12. Last Days in Kiev 129
  13. Glasnost-Perestroika:
     Open Door or Window Dressing?............ 139
EPILOGUE 147
APPENDIX....................................... 149

PREFACE

All of our meetings and partings
are set in heaven.
(Saying of Russian believers)

Like many Russian writers (well, perhaps not just Russian
ones) I've had the goal of writing a very weighty, serious, and
profound book. My ambition was that the resulting master-
piece would bring about a change in humanity's perceptions, or
at least, in a significant part of it. The characters in the book,
together with the author, were to experience Dostoyevskian
sufferings, arguments, and heart-burnings on every one of its
many pages. But God gave this ambition another twist.

In ten years of life in America, I have published many stories and articles but never got around to writing my planned
magnum opus. Instead of that, I have published other people's
books. I cannot say that this has caused me any regrets, for I
am certain that the dozens of books which I have published
have been of use to readers in Russia.

But now, ten years later, after an unexpected trip to the
Soviet Union, I have written my book. Upon my return, it
poured out like a short but strong July shower. This book is
still not the major work "à la Dostoyevsky" that I had once
hoped to write, but the notes of a traveler, written down
immediately on return.

In this book, I have tried to depict Russia as I saw her after
an absence of ten years. This encounter can be likened to a
return to one's first love. Every one of us has had a first love,

though few of us bind our lives to it forever. Nevertheless, the delicate fragrance of youth and that first love remain with us for the rest of our days. We fall in love again, we join our lives with others, we raise children, but if we chance to encounter our first love, our hearts start to beat with a sweet and quickened tempo, just as they did years before.

I hope that my voice will not be the only one heard in this work, but that the voices of the people I met will also speak. Their voices are the voices of contemporary Russia, a nation in the process of forging her destiny, on which, I believe, hangs the destiny of the rest of the world. I would like to thank every reader for embarking with me on my journey and ask everyone to pray for this great country with her tragic fate and unknown future.

WESTERN RUSSIA

Miles	0		100	200	300	400	500
Kms	0	200	400		600	800	

▬▬ U.S.S.R. national boundary   ● Cities

-·-·-·- National boundaries   ★ National capital

··········· Boundaries of Soviet Socialist Republics   ○ S.S.R. capitals

INTRODUCTION

You meet by the clothes;
you part by the mind.
(Russian saying)

For a writer, just as for the lover trying to explain his feelings after falling in love, the first words are the hardest. I hope you will understand my problem, for I am meeting so many of you all at once. Therefore, I invite you, my readers, to take the necessary steps to get to know me.

My name is Mikhail Morgulis. I often joke that Mikhail Gorbachev and I share the same forename, but have different jobs. He works for the Communists, while I work for Christ. Yet there was a time when I believed, quite sincerely, that human ideas could be sufficient to make mankind happy. Like millions of Soviet citizens I believed that man is the master of his own destiny. But you and I know, do we not, that people cannot be the total masters of their fates, no matter how hard they try. They may labor diligently and stubbornly to forge their own happiness, but despite this, their eyes are frequently filled with tears. The answer to this is simple—we all have a heavenly Master in whose hands our fates lie. He, alone, is the source of true peace and lasting happiness.

So who am I? First, I was a Soviet child, a Soviet schoolboy, a Soviet university student, a Soviet writer, and a Soviet journalist. In many respects, my life followed the usual pattern shared by the majority of Russians. But there came a time when my soul began to ail and to ache. I recall a line out of a favorite poem: "The soul, like a bird, seeks bread." At that time, my soul was hungering after spiritual bread.

My path to God was a difficult one. I fell, was hurt, and wounded as I slowly moved toward His comfort. Even after knowing of God, it took me two years to reach Him. I faltered and turned back, yet invariably returned once more to that difficult path. I remember the glorious day when my heart suddenly brimmed over with love, and I said to Him, "Lord, forgive my sins and bless me with Your love. You see all that is in my heart, so there is no need for me to say anything else." I recall well my simple proselyte's plea: "Bless me with Your love; bless me with Your purity; bless me with joys and sorrows; bless me, and be with me always."

It was by the blue waters of Ashford Lake in Connecticut that I entered into my covenant with God. I remember that bright, sunny day so clearly. I stood there, looking up into the pale-blue wash of the sky, and it seemed to me as though Someone's eyes looked down upon me with love.

Before America, there was the ordeal of emigrating from Russia. This was followed by all the complexities of living as a refugee. It was during this time that I began to read the Bible, a gift from an American missionary. As I read, I sensed the echo of history deep within myself. I understood and identified with the characters of the Bible, both Old and New Testaments. The message of God's love for humanity became plainly evident to me in the pages of His Word. At that time I promised myself, "Never, never shall I be without this book."

With life in America came joys and sorrows. I worked with Russian language papers, journals, and radio stations. Everything seemed to be working out well, but the Lord had a different plan. He said to leave everything and follow Him. I was to serve Him alone. I hesitated, but God showed me His will, and I went to serve Him at Slavic Gospel Press in Wheaton, Illinois.

My job in Wheaton involves translating and publishing books for a Russian audience. I am also busy taping two daily Russian radio broadcasts: "Back to God," which is a translation of Dr. Joel Nederhood's "The Back to God Hour," and a program which I write myself, "New Life," produced by Rev. Alex Leonovich. Both programs have millions of listeners in the Soviet Union, and I receive hundreds of letters from them.

Ten years after I left Russia, a group of American Christians invited me to accompany them on a trip to the Soviet Union. The organizer of this trip was RACOM Associates, a non-profit corporation that supports "The Back to God Hour" (a ministry of the Christian Reformed Church).

This book is about that trip. I must warn you, however, that it is not strictly documentary in nature. I ask my readers' understanding, in that I was returning to the land of my child-hood and youth, where every stone, every tree, every en-counter would awaken numerous associations from the past. That is why I so often swing between events of the present and the past. Still, I think this may even help you, my readers, for you will get a better feel and grasp of that immense, enig-matic planet which I call "Russia" through the prism of one man's heart. Hundreds of specialists have written analytical tomes about Russia, but in most cases they focus on the su-perficial "Russian life and soul" subject matter. Yet, beneath the visible surface there is an amazing, vital life, a life which is simultaneously frightening and fascinating. And it is this that I want to show you.

We were 35 Americans landing on the 285 million-strong Red Planet. Most of the inhabitants of this planet spoke Rus-sian. In our group, the only Russian speakers were my six-teen-year-old daughter and me. But most of us saw ourselves as emissaries of Christ, so we ventured forward with a smile and a prayer.

We were not a tourist group in the strict sense of the word. We wanted to find out what *perestroika* (restructuring) and *glasnost* (openness) had given the country and how it had af-fected religious believers. Apart from that, I had my own hopes and plans, which nobody knew or even suspected, not even my daughter. They were known only to myself and to God. By the time you finish reading this book, you too will know what they were.

Well, now we have been introduced. You know a little about

me, soon to discover more. Don't worry, I believe I know you already. I feel that I have come to know you quite well in the ten years I have lived in America. I see your friendly faces in the streets, churches, and homes of my neighborhood. I see the warmth in your eyes and your smiles. I think we'll make compatible traveling companions. You'll be going on a trip, not only through Russia, but through one man's soul. As you read these pages you'll travel through my thoughts, feelings, and emotions. I invite you to settle down comfortably, and let us begin our journey to the Red Planet.

CHAPTER ONE

My Return on a River of Memories

What is a memory? It is a river of
tears with islands of happiness.
(From a Morgulis short story)

August 2, 1988 . . .

I left Russia ten years ago. At that time I stopped being one of
her citizens, and became one of her scattered refugees. The
Motherland released me reluctantly, like a sword being drawn
from her belly. It was like a reenactment of a situation frequently encountered in life—you don't care for something, but
you are still unwilling to give it up. At that time, many were
convinced—including the KGB—that I was taking a foolhardy,
unwarranted step.

This conviction was aired to me by senior Party "comrades"
in the literary and cultural world. I was told this by a very
intelligent-looking KGB major who confronted me saying,
"Comrade Morgulis, you have achieved quite a lot. You're
thirty-five years old, and already an author and playwright.
Your stories and articles are published in the press without
hindrance, not to mention your earnings, which are considera-
bly higher than many Soviet people. And don't forget that in
1972, the state awarded you first prize in a writers' contest.[1]

---

[1] All he said was true. That year, the Soviet Writers' Union and the Ministry of Culture
had conducted a literary competition. The cash prizes offered were quite high. I was
told some 600 writers from all over the Soviet Union submitted entries. The Soviet
literary system had decided to exhibit its "democratic nature" on this occasion and
judged the entries without knowing the authors' names.

The system's gamble did not pay off. The jury was unanimous in declaring my
entry to be the winning one, so the author of the first prize turned out to be

The major continued, "Yet despite all this, you want to leave! And I had always thought of you as a clever person. Don't you understand that you will find yourself in a place where nobody knows you or needs you? You can't imagine what hardships you will have to face in America."

I felt it prudent to remain silent, for it was impossible to respond with the truth, and as for lies—well, I had had enough of those. I was once again reminded of the truth inherent in the old saying, "Speech is silver, but silence is golden." So I confined myself to a short reply, "Even if I do encounter hardships, I don't see how that is anybody's business but my own."

At the end of our meeting, the major sighed hypocritically and responded, "I regret that I can give you no assurances that you will find yourself in America soon. In fact, it may be that your train will head for Siberia instead."

I was unable to explain to the major (or perhaps even fully to myself) that I was being moved by a mighty, unseen force which was driving me out of a comfortable, but slave-like existence. I burned with a desire to see the world, which is forbidden territory to the majority of Soviet citizens. I wanted to begin a journey to see the world and to find that which I had been subconsciously seeking all my life. At that time I had not yet reached the firm belief that all our meetings and partings, our joys and our sorrows are determined on high.

I was eventually given permission to leave the Soviet Union. It would take too long to relate all that went on in my heart at that time; suffice to say that I was leaving one life, and plunging into the uncharted territory of another.

I left behind the places of my childhood and youth, places which remain intact in my heart and are independent of any political system. I left seeing the beloved and apprehensive eyes of my mother and the genuine concern of my relatives, not knowing whether I would ever look on them again. I was

---

not some "establishment" writer, but a young and unknown author, and one who had a habit of attending Party meetings wearing a pair of American jeans. There was considerable confusion, but the newspapers had to publish the results nonetheless. The money I won was enough to keep me and my friends partying for several months.

flying off to a distant planet, into the future, and what that future held was a mystery.

A Childhood of Innocence Lost

Yet now, ten years later, I was returning to my Red Planet, into my past. To the accompaniment of the steady droning of the airplane engines, I recalled various episodes of my life. A river of memories flooded my mind.

Here I am, age two. Russia was at war with Nazi Germany. Our house had been bombed, so we had to live in a dugout. By day, my cousin Mark, age four, and I were alone.

Once a shell exploded right near the dugout, making it cave in. The homemade stove teetered perilously, parts of the ceiling began to sag. Mark seized me by the hand and dragged me into a niche in the dugout wall, shaking with fear. When the adults returned, they put up a terrible clamor, thinking we had died under the ruins. I recall the desperate, drawn-out screams of my mother. On that occasion I learned that death, like a caring nurse, walks alongside us from our earliest days.

Mark always had a tendency to remind me jokingly that he had saved my life. Dear Mark, is it really ten years since I last saw you?

Suddenly another memory; I am age three. The Soviet army was already battling on the territory of Nazi-occupied Europe. My officer father was a Communist, but one of those romantic followers who really believed that Communism could finally bring happiness to mankind. Other fathers sent their families food parcels, silverware, and carpets from Europe. But my father sent us pencils, stating proudly that real Communists never take what is not theirs, instructing Mother to teach me the alphabet. I remember tantalizing odors of warm meat conserves floating out of neighbors' windows while I sat there, my mouth watering, and sharpened pencils with a blunt kitchen knife.

After the war, when my father realized that Marxist dreams of universal well-being were nothing but "soap bubbles of blood" and that Soviet life was, in reality, governed by cynics, pragmatists, and liars, he retreated into a strange kind of self-imposed solitude for the rest of his life. Only once, not long before he died from the wounds he had received during the war, did he say to me, "If I had my life to live over again, I would live it differently."

As the engines droned on, another memory emerged. World War II finally ended. Russia was among the victors. No longer were there Russian prisoners working in German factories, but now German prisoners were employed in the rebuilding of the Russian cities they had bombed. The house we lived in was being reconstructed by a brigade of prisoners of war. The residents of the house were hostile to them. After all, very few families emerged unscathed from the war without death or injury. The gang of prisoner-laborers kept saying over and over, "Hitler bad! Hitler kaput!"

I was five years old and I felt sorry for them—especially one old peasant who had four children back in Germany. Like everyone else, we had very little of anything, but at times I was able to sneak him a potato or a bit of bread or onion. In return he gave me roasted bits of corn out of a small leather pouch. (I still can't figure out where he got that corn.) Once my mother saw them and took them away from me immediately, thinking that they might have been poisoned. On another occasion one of our neighbors saw me giving Hans, the German peasant, a bit of bread.

"How can you give them anything?" she yelled. "They killed your three uncles! How can you feel sorry for them?"

I began to cry and tried to explain, "I don't know why I feel sorry for them, but I do."

Many years later, when I was sixteen, that same neighbor once asked me, "Why did you pity those Germans?"

And again, the only thing I could say was, "I don't know why, I just did."

As the plane continued its trek, my mind continued on mine. When I was six, older children explained to me how babies were made and how I had come into existence. This was a painful disclosure. For a long time I could not even look at my parents. I felt that they, whom I had always considered to be good and pure, had somehow cheated and betrayed me. How important it is that we should learn delicate, intimate secrets from those we love and to whom we are close, and not from the foul mouths of strangers.

A Night of Vision

Then from the deep recesses of my mind I recalled another image. One night in 1950 something woke me, and I looked out the window. Several people were leading a neighbor of ours to a black car. I knew that he had been arrested. In those years millions of people were arrested at night. They lived in dread of the knock on the door in darkness. I imagine that my father too expected to be taken away.

The neighbor moved as though his legs were made of wood. And then, as if he felt my eyes on him, he raised his head and looked straight up at my window. By the colorless light of the moon I saw that his face was frozen into a mask of fear. His eyes were filled with silent entreaty. For a long time afterward I was regularly haunted by his terrifying eyes and face, frozen into a desperate, Pierrot-like mask. In fact, I have remembered this chilling moment all of my life.

Stalin died in 1953, when I was going on eleven years old. I stood crying before the ancient black radio. I was not alone in my tears—many wept over the man who was responsible for the deaths of millions of people. At that time, I was unable to understand my grandmother's whispered comment: "It is good people for whom you should weep."

With each passing moment, the memories continued to flow. A streetcar knocked over and killed a boy from our school. He lay there dying, in the middle of the road, pinkish bubbles coming from his mouth. He was not a nice boy: he stole and bullied those who were weaker than he. But as he lay there, his life draining out of him, there was nobody in the world dearer or closer to me than he.

I realized that it is wrong to feel pleasure at someone's death, even that of an evil person. For we are all human, and each death diminishes us too. I have hated the color pink ever since that day.

Still more thoughts stirred. I fell in love for the first time when I was thirteen. She had green eyes, and this color of hope became my favorite forevermore. We were racing around, playing tag, when she twisted her ankle and fell. I bent over her, looking into her pain-filled green eyes. For the first time in my life I sincerely wished that another's pain would transfer itself to me.

I said to her, "When I grow up I'm going to be a sailor, marry you, and take you far, far away."

Well, I did not become a sailor, nor did I take her away. In fact, I forgot all about her quite soon, but I have never forgotten that wonderful feeling—the desire to take on somebody else's pain. Perhaps this is what love is—the desire to share the pain of the beloved.

My mind continued to wander as I remembered a classmate who used to stick pins into butterflies and watch their sufferings. I was horrified at his actions.

"Why do you do that?" I demanded. "It's like driving a stake through them! What for?"

He only laughed, and I said with conviction, "The person who does something like this can die the same death."

I met him some twenty-one years later. His wife, whom he adored, had left him. His suffering and jealousy tortured him day and night. He had started to drink heavily. Finally he committed suicide by jumping out of a sixth-floor window. I would not claim that such retribution invariably catches up with those who deliberately inflict pain. But it happens often enough. Especially to those who torture people.

I often ponder the eternal fate of those who so callously participated in the Stalinist purges. How can they sleep?

Finally, as the plane was landing in Moscow I recalled my first encounter, as an adult, with religious believers. It happened at a small, country railway station in Russia. A man in an ill-fitting suit began to talk to me about God. I laughed at him. He said that he would pray for me and my future. Who knows, maybe it was by his prayers that God directed my footsteps through the Egyptian desert to the land of Canaan. I wondered where are you now, my nameless benefactor.

All these thoughts and more went through my mind as I

returned to my native land. How ironic it was that the flight to my home was also a journey to the center of my mind. The river of memories was a perfect preparation for the travels yet to come.

CHAPTER TWO

Return to the Red Planet

Life brings us two kinds of sur-
prises, bad and very bad. In any
case, trust the Lord.
(Old Russian saying)

August 2–3, 1988 . . .

You can't go home again, I've heard it said. That may well be
true, for even if the land had only changed a little, I had
changed a lot through the years. Any changes in Russia remained to be seen—that was the purpose of my trip. The
changes in my life were certain and sure. Here I was, a man
who had left Russia as a recent member of the Communist
Youth League (Komsomol), an atheist, and a Soviet journalist,
now returning as a witness for Christ.

I had changed a great deal in the intervening years, but the
most important change was that I had left Russia as a proud
darling of fate who wanted to see the world, but was returning
as the servant of the Nazarene.

Our delegation of thirty-five Americans of varying profes-
sions and ages was bound together by a common faith in God.
Though we came from different backgrounds, we quickly assimilated into a tight-knit tour group.

Naturally, I could not help feeling nervous about the whole
trip. In the first instance, everyone in the group had received
their entry visas without any problems, but mine came through
only a few hours before the flight. The Soviet authorities were
giving a silent demonstration of their attitude toward this
"prodigal son." There was another cause for serious concern—we had some 700 Russian Bibles with us, as well as

other Christian literature. How would things go in customs? How real would Gorbachev's reforms turn out to be in practice? But sitting in the plane I made a firm resolution to conceal nothing from start to finish. I would make no attempt to either fool or mislead the authorities.

Customs: Search or Seizure?

Typically, the same psychological scenario is enacted over and over again in Soviet customs. Luggage is checked by about fifteen customs officials, with each one having a line to his or her desk. As might be expected, the shrewd traveler will try to stand in the line of the most cheerful and friendly-looking official.

There are unwritten recommendations which advise against going to a woman official if it can be avoided—especially a young one. If she wears a *Komsomol* badge on her jacket, she is to be skipped. Flying in the face of such advice, I deliberately went to a young woman, complete with badge. She was clearly from one of the Soviet Central Asian republics, where there are more than 50 million Muslims. Her slanted eyes surveyed the newly arrived passengers without a spark of warmth. There was no line leading to her desk.

I thought, This is my first test, Lord, and stepped toward her.

"Do you have any forbidden literature?" was her first question, in English.

"You can speak Russian—it's my mother tongue," I responded.

She raised the dark slits of her eyes, and I saw in them something that I already knew: the Soviet system particularly dislikes having to receive those who have had the temerity to leave it. People like me were referred to, until quite recently, as deserters and traitors. Now, under Gorbachev, it is said that something is changing. At least, that is the opinion of American newspaper correspondents in Moscow. Furthermore, several "liberal" Soviet journals, which act as Gorbachev's mouthpieces, have begun to hint as much. Admittedly, quite a lot of émigrés have been able to travel back to

Russia in recent times to see their relatives. So it was with interest that I waited to see whether this alleged new attitude was to be seen in Soviet customs, as well as on the pages of its newspapers.

She repeated the question in Russian, sounding for all the world like a talking robot, "Do you have any prohibited literature?"

"Nothing that's prohibited, only that which is permitted," I shot back at her.

"What do you call 'permitted literature'?" she questioned.

I answered, "The kind that the laws of your country don't forbid—Bibles, for instance. But you don't have to search for them; they're in that suitcase."

I opened the suitcase, which contained about 100 Bibles, New Testaments, cassettes of my radio programs, and 600 postcards with biblical texts. Among all this lay a copy of Gorbachev's recent book *Perestroika and Glasnost,* with his portrait on the cover.

"We can't let a quantity like that go through," she said firmly. "Only two Bibles per head are allowed in." And then she noticed the Gorbachev book. "Why did you put that in here?" she asked.

"In case there was any trouble here in customs about the Bibles," I replied frankly. "Your leader is always writing and saying that in this time of *glasnost,* there are no restrictions on the import of religious literature into the Soviet Union. It looks to me as though the General Secretary of the Communist Party of the USSR says one thing, and you do another. How can this be?"

Gorbachev Comes to Help

The officials occupying the nearby tables sensed trouble and hurried over to assist their colleague.

"Why are you refusing to surrender the proscribed literature and cassettes?" the most senior official demanded in a deep bass voice.

"I would have no objections to surrendering prohibited literature," I responded, adding, "but would you kindly show me the article of the Constitution which forbids the import of Bibles!"

Of course, I knew that there is no such article in the Constitution, but I knew equally well that there was a secret instruction issued by the KGB to that effect, and unwritten orders can have the force of law. Since much is changing now in Soviet Society, I thought it worthwhile to test their stand.

The senior official was annoyed. "You're too smart," he grumbled. "You think you know all the laws."

"I don't consider myself at all clever," I retorted. "I just want to give people Bibles. You say that I know all the laws, but I must say that I don't know of any law forbidding the import of religious literature."

At this point, we were joined by a tall, energetic-looking man who was the head of the customs service. He ordered at once, "If it's something trivial, let it pass. Take away only that which is important."

"Quite right," I chipped in. "I'm really being delayed over trivia." Then I sighed theatrically and added, "Thank God somebody here has read Gorbachev's book!"

His jaw dropped at my words. I opened the book at random and gave it to him saying, "Gorbachev writes that now, in the era of *glasnost*, religious literature may be brought into the country freely, but it looks as though none of your subordinates have read his book."

They quickly responded with assurances that they had indeed read Gorbachev's opus. But I could tell by their faces that they were lying. And I must confess that I was not certain that Gorbachev had written something like that in the book.

In order to keep up the pressure, I played my trump card and pulled out a letter from the Chairman of the Council for Religious Affairs of the USSR, Konstantin Kharchev—a senior Party member responsible for religious life in the country. In that letter Kharchev consented to giving me an interview during my stay in Moscow.

While the letter was being perused with considerable awe by the others, my customs official did not give up.

"Was it you who supplied the rest of your group with religious literature?" she demanded sourly.

I was tempted to say no, but came out with a firm yes instead, responding, "You must understand that they are all religious believers, and if they had not received the books from me, they would have got them from someone else. They are morally prepared for the consequences." And then I went on, lowering my voice even more, "What kind of presents do you expect Christians to bring for their fellow believers in another country? You know we don't bring in pornographic literature or other forbidden material. We feel that a Bible is the best gift of all."

The senior official returned Kharchev's letter, and striving to speak in firm, commanding tones, ordered, "Let through everything except a quarter of the postcards and ten out of the fifty cassettes."

"Why a quarter of the postcards and ten of the cassettes?" I demanded immediately.

"Because," he answered triumphantly, "those postcards have biblical texts on them. If someone puts a postage stamp on them, they automatically qualify as religious propaganda. And religious propaganda, as you know, is forbidden by law in our country. The same goes for the cassettes. You should realize that we are being very loyal in our behavior toward you. In other cases we would confiscate the lot, but we're accommodating you."

His logic was questionable, but they had to clearly show their authority in some way, and would make no further concessions. I did some quick mental arithmetic, and was not displeased. A quarter out of 600 postcards would leave me with 450. And along with my 40 remaining cassettes, there were about 100 more scattered throughout our group. So I raised no more objections. Moreover, they wrote out a receipt, with which I could claim the confiscated material on my way back out of Russia. I was left with all my Bibles and New Testaments, a good stack of postcards, the cassettes, and other odds and ends. Preparing to move on, I said, "God bless you!" loudly to all of them, but made a point of looking directly at the young woman. Several of the officials grinned sourly, but the others did not react at all to my farewell.

The young woman shrugged irritably and snarled, "There's no need for that nonsense."

"I'm sorry you feel that way," I said, "but that is the best possible thing I could wish anyone."

Ed Schierbeek, the leader of our tour group, was waiting for me at the exit. I immediately flashed him the victory sign. The rest of the group was already in the "Intourist" bus. They had been waiting for me for about an hour.

I hurried to tell the group the good news. "Everything's all right, thank God!" I exclaimed, boarding the bus. They burst into applause. During the entire time I had been delayed in customs they had all been praying for me. This was but the first of many evidences of God's hand working in my life during the trip.

A Black Market Revelation

I kept thinking about customs as the bus moved off. It is no secret that confiscated goods regularly find their way from customs onto the black market. Videos, cassettes, records, cameras, radio equipment, and books—all of these fetch astronomical black market prices. For instance, a blank video cassette is worth around 75 rubles, whereas a video cassette of an American show, from 150 to 200 rubles, the equivalent of the monthly salary of an engineer, a teacher, or doctor. Unfortunately, even Bibles, Christian literature, and Christian radio and video cassettes have black market value by reason of their scarcity. One Bible, for example, can cost anywhere from 60 to 200 rubles.

Later, at the entrance to the hotel, I was approached by a black marketer offering various Bibles for sale, including those published by us at the Slavic Gospel Association. Indeed, there was even one farcical incident when a black marketer offered to sell me some cassettes with my own radio programs on them! I told him that he was asking too much, but then to my slight chagrin the black marketer offered to let me buy "me" at a lower price. I couldn't pass up his price. The cassettes turned out to be copies of the original cassettes made by me in the United States. There must be a market for them if they're making and selling copies. After all, the black market is not a charitable institute, and it doesn't handle anything that is not in demand. It was admittedly a strange channel, but one by which the Gospel was going out to the ends of the earth, in Russia anyway.

Of course, Soviet customs is not the only source for Western religious materials coming onto the black market. There are other avenues, but customs is a major supplier to illegal businesses.

CHAPTER THREE

Moscow: City of Meetings and Mysteries

Moscow does not believe in tears.
(Russian saying)

August 3–4, 1988 . . .

Upon arriving in Moscow we stayed in the large and rather dirty *Rossiya* Hotel, known for its secret presence in each room. In the *Rossiya,* just as in all Soviet hotels where foreigners stay, there are hidden listening devices. I knew about this from various reliable sources even before I left the Soviet Union. I decided to test their surveillance tactics in my capacity as a visiting "foreigner." Who knows, I thought, maybe *perestroika* had wrought some significant social changes in my homeland.

To test the policy, I sent along one of my Russian friends to have a word with the manager of the hotel, a person who, as my friend remarked with dour humor, would sell his grandmother for a bribe. The conversation between them went as follows:

My friend: "There's an American friend of mine who wants to change his room for a better one, and he's willing to pay the difference in dollars."

Manager: "The rooms are available, and we need dollars, but (deep sigh) I can't let him change. The KGB wouldn't permit it, because those rooms aren't bugged."

My conclusion: *Perestroika* definitely goes on, but plainly not everywhere, and certainly not in the KGB's sphere of activity.

My Plan of Attack

Moscow is huge, noisy, fast-moving, and bewildering to the newcomer, just like all large cities the world over. The present population is about 8 million (larger than New York City) and even though it is popularly called a "big village," it is rather like a small country.

On the day of arrival I promised myself not to sleep more than two to three hours a night, and to use the time saved to meet as many people as possible. It was a hectic pace. But I must say that I stuck to this promise. There were times when I did not sleep at all for a couple of nights in a row.

My meetings, observations, and discussions took place on three levels:

• 1st level: With well-known government officials, who occupy important posts;

• 2nd level: With friends and acquaintances scattered throughout the social spectrum, but mainly highly educated people (the intelligentsia), who trusted me;

• 3rd level: With people in the street, those encountered by chance, such as taxi drivers and militiamen.

There was also a fourth, special sphere—the religious one, which brought me into contact with ideologues responsible for overseeing religion in the USSR. I also met with pastors, priests, and churchgoers of both registered churches and unregistered churches, with representatives of the new, so-called Autonomous church, with representatives of "house churches," as well as with monks, and Christian musical groups and singers.

Meeting with such a wide spectrum of people gave me some opportunities to interact with people from the whole of Russian culture. This unique blend of people gave me a true sense of the changes rippling through the waters of Soviet society.

Takin' It to the Streets

We arrived in Moscow in the evening, but pursuing the strategy I had mapped out in advance, I did not stop to rest, but called up some friends, met them, and set off to wandering around Moscow.

There are always plenty of black marketers, prostitutes, and plainclothesmen from the militia and the KGB around the *Rossiya*. It's not easy to catch a taxi in Moscow, but there is never any shortage of them by the *Rossiya*, and the drivers name their price immediately, usually three to five times the regular fare. This too is a reflection of socialism: do what you will, there's no competition anyway. The taxi drivers all agree that taking prostitutes to assignations is a very profitable line of business.

The American reader may find it hard to believe that in the center of the "blue stocking"—Moscow—are plenty of hives of prostitution, drug abuse, and alcoholism, which are totally unaffected by Gorbachev's initiatives and all the prohibitions arising out of them. The militia and the hotel security staff typically turn a blind eye to such illicit activities because they get their "cut" from the businesses. These are not simply my speculations. I knew about these problems before; the extent of their rampage was only reaffirmed by the Muscovites whom I happened to question about it. Incidentally, the more liberal Moscow press has recently begun to air these social evils more openly.

The most interesting discussions I had were with taxi drivers. They've seen it all, they're cynical, curious, and up to date with all the current events. Taxi drivers the world over, it seems, are frequently good judges of people.

That evening, a taxi took us to visit an elderly woman, a believer to whom I had to give a parcel from her friends in the USA. We got talking with the driver along the way. I expressed the opinion that Gorbachev would finally overcome the complex web of clandestine corruption.

The driver shook his head and disagreed, "No, he won't. He may be able to do away with it in one place, like Uzbekistan, for instance, but he has no chance of stamping it out in the country as a whole. Corruption's like a cancer, and we have no way of curing it. He can't win because corruption feeds everyone. Money and Western goods—these are the most important things to those who are corrupt. None of them are going to let go, even under threat of prison, because practicing corruption is the key to an 'easy' life in the generally very difficult conditions of Soviet existence."

Spirits of the Black Market

In Moscow I learned much from life in the streets. Foreign goods, especially American ones, are in enormous demand. One pack of Marlboro cigarettes can fetch 10 rubles (that's $16 according to the official rate of exchange). Cigarettes manufactured in the Soviet Union retail at 30 to 40 kopecks a pack (that is, from 50 to 60¢ in America). American jeans are far and away the favorite market item—one pair costs 200–250 rubles ($320–370). These are amazing figures when you consider that a Soviet citizen's average monthly income is from 120 to 180 rubles.

There is also a flourishing black market trade in alcohol, which has been stimulated by Gorbachev's anti-drinking campaign. Vodka is now made at home. Earlier, "moonshine" was made mainly by the lower strata of society, mainly peasants, but now it has become a widespread phenomenon in the cities. Moonshine vodka is distilled by engineers, artists, and scientists. As a result, the technology of home brewing and distillation (unlike its industrial counterpart) has progressed by leaps and bounds.

The Russian people have never lost their sense of humor under any circumstances, nor have they lost it now. Therefore, these home brews are usually given exotic names such as "Domestic Gorbachevka," "Raisa's Dreams," or "Cognac Mikhail."

A direct result of the upsurge in illegal alcohol production has been the disappearance of sugar from all the shops. The amateur brewers have scooped it up in huge amounts. Thus, the state had to introduce rationing of sugar. As for the vodka produced legally in state factories, it immediately became a black market commodity. At the same time, chemists were cleaned out of cheap eaux de cologne and all medicines with a spirit base. They were bought up by alcoholics. So now in the chemist shops, just as in liquor stores, eau de cologne is not sold in the mornings. The aim of this is to stop people from drinking before they go to work.

Soviet statisticians have been forced to acknowledge that millions of industrial accidents have been caused by drunkenness. There are ghastly incidents of people being pulled into machines and falling into vats filled with acid. There have been injuries, burns, loss of limbs, hearing, and sight.

Yet despite all official measures, Russia continues to drink. Thousands of deaths have been caused by the drinking of furniture polish, detergents, and various industrial compounds containing spirit. However, it seems that Gorbachev and his supporters have come to realize that sobriety cannot be enforced, so the liquor stores have begun to sell more wines. It is patently obvious that this terrible malaise, which has become a national epidemic, cannot be wiped out by government decrees. You cannot, overnight, expunge the habits of centuries which have become daily practices—almost the norm rather than an exception.

The church has offered a helping hand to the state in this matter, but so far the state has chosen to ignore it. The state's thinking is understandable. To accept the assistance of the church is to acknowledge its influence on human life, and at the same time, to acknowledge government's impotence. Nonetheless, in recent times religious believers have occasionally been allowed to visit hospitals where chronic alcoholics are treated. It must be noted that believers have regularly offered help to hospital personnel free of charge. On one hand, the state needs such help desperately, because there is a drastic shortage of nursing assistance but on the other, the state shies away from what it calls "religious propaganda."

For instance, believers in Moscow offered to help tend the patients in the hospital near their church. This was to be without remuneration. The authorities suffered some uncertainty and finally came up with a compromise: they gave permission for the believers to assist in a psychiatric clinic for violent patients. One can clearly see the appearance of propriety this compromise would have in the West. However, though the believers were not refused, there is not likely to be much effective "religious propaganda" in a place full of

"Christs," "Napoleons," and "Hitlers." This is a classic example of the cool, calculated compromises made by the Soviet authorities.

The Evolution of Kharchev

The following day I phoned the Council for Religious Affairs, the state watchdog body over religious life in the land. I had written to its head, Konstantin Kharchev, before coming to Russia. In his last letter, he informed me that he was preparing to go on holiday to Karlovy Vary in Czechoslovakia, and suggested that we meet in Moscow another time. But my trip was already booked. I couldn't change it, even though I knew that Kharchev was not to be in Moscow. I spoke to his deputy, who passed on Kharchev's regards and desire to meet me for a discussion. She then suggested that I take an interview from one of Kharchev's deputies, but I preferred to wait for a meeting with the "Gorbachev of religion" himself.

I already knew something about him. Before he took up his present post in the Council for Religious Affairs, he was a diplomat and was posted as Soviet ambassador to countries in Africa. There is no doubt that he is a committed Communist, who has been appointed by the Party to this difficult post. He grew up an orphan, and is fond of stressing that he owes his education and his career to the Party. Yet nevertheless, I have observed some very positive features amid his cynical, pragmatic, and atheistic approach to life, I would even say—pleasant features: he has shown friendly concern to strangers, a desire to help the sick and the young, and—may his enemies forgive me!—a certain compassion which he tries to conceal. (The Appendix of this book provides a transcript of a secretly taped address he delivered to the Higher Party School of the USSR.)

In the six months between the 19th Party conference and the speech, there has been a noticeable change in Kharchev's position. In the interview he calls openly for equal rights for believers and nonbelievers in the Soviet Union, for the rescinding of the shameful requirement of registration of churches. I do not think this metamorphosis has come about by chance, but due to the winds of change of *glasnost* and the personal influence of Gorbachev, who is a good friend of his. It seems to me that in the years Kharchev has worked with believers, he has come to view them with respect and a degree of sympathy. He is far from accepting their views, but it seems to me that he has gained a better understanding of the moral values of Christianity, and, moreover, I should think of the person and work of Christ.

The Pentecostal Exodus

During the day I had scheduled a meeting with leaders of the unregistered Soviet Pentecostals, who number around 1 million members. Extreme precautions were taken so that our secret encounter would not be uncovered. The Pentecostal bishop and I finally came together at a clandestine rendezvous in the center of Moscow.

The Pentecostal movement of emigration for religious reasons is gaining strength in the Soviet Union. The Soviet authorities have already allowed several thousand Pentecostals to leave for the West, around 30,000 more have lodged applications for exit visas, and an even greater number is thinking of emigrating. I believe there is a move toward a mass exodus of this denomination from the USSR. Incidentally, there are signs of a similar move among Soviet Baptists in recent times. As is to be expected, believers have split into two factions on this matter: those who wish to emigrate, and those who wish to remain.

Concerned about this issue, I addressed several direct questions to the Pentecostal leaders: "What is the idea behind your emigration campaign? Does it have a spiritual significance? After all, many say: 'If all the faithful emigrate, who shall spread the Word of God to the people?' Do you find support in the Bible for your decisions? Hasn't the situation of believers improved markedly under Gorbachev? So why don't the Pentecostals strive for the legalization of their churches?"[1]

---

[1]Several months later Kharchev, presumably expressing the thinking of Gorbachev and his supporters, called for the rescinding of the requirement of compulsory registration of religious communities. However, to this day this has not been implemented.

The senior Pentecostal bishop, Ivan Fedotov, replied to my questions. Fedotov had just recently been released from imprisonment, where he had spent a total of nineteen years for his religious convictions. He is an extremely forceful personality, very strict and businesslike; like all Russian Protestants he dresses very simply, usually in dark colors, and wears no ties or accessories. He was accompanied by his wife, who, like most women of her kind, always stood a few paces behind him, a scarf about her head, and took no part in the conversation of the men. This is a typical submissive posture for them.

"With regard to emigration," said Fedotov, "we wish to bring up our children in the faith. We do not believe that the relaxations that we see at the moment are permanent. We feel that this time of *grace* will be followed by one of *persecution*. For the same reason, we are not seeking registration of our communities—we do not believe that the authorities will keep their promises. We do not want to face arrests, as we have in the past, when the situation in the Soviet Union goes into reverse. And, in any case, even if we were to register, the authorities would still try to bring us under their 'spiritual' control by some means or other. They would soon start trying to foist 'their' leaders on to us. No, the body of the church is not a chicken for them to pluck, leaving us with nothing but the feathers. We believe that the Lord is pointing us toward Exodus. We cannot foretell the future, but we believe that all is being done in accordance with the Word of God. We have borne persecution too long, we have spent too many years in prisons, to believe that there is any good future awaiting our children here."

Fedotov was an elegant spokesman for his people. Listening to him, I realized the difficult decision that Soviet Pentecostals face. With my brief visit to the Pentecostals complete, I moved on.

Paper on Fire
In my travels I also met Vera Godayeva and Vladimir Kulikov, members of the editorial team of the *Bratsky Vestnik* (Fraternal Herald), the only officially permitted evangelical journal in

the USSR. The journal provides some interesting information, but the print run is very small—approximately 5,000 copies. And even so, the majority of each issue goes to Russian readers in the West.

Vera Godayeva was the first believer to have appeared on Soviet television. Addressing early-morning viewers, preparing to go to work, she provided a witness by calling on them to avoid being unpleasant to others on public transport, to smile at each other, and not to blame others for the inconveniences of crammed trains and buses. "If you do just this," she regularly told them, "you will see what a pleasant day you will have!"

While talking with believers, I also learned of another upstart publishing endeavor. In fact, even as this book goes to press, young Christians in the Soviet Union have begun publication of a paper called *The Protestant*. It is an unofficial publication, and is financed entirely by its keen and energetic young publishers. The print run is tiny, of course, but it is effective nonetheless, because young believers faithfully circulate it among themselves.

In the current climate of *glasnost* this has become a possibility, for although the authorities delay issuing official permission, they do not, at the same time, close such printing projects down. Nobody can say, of course, how long such a state of affairs will last. Until new government legislation is passed concerning the publication of papers and journals by private persons, all the unofficial publications which have sprung up in recent times could be closed down overnight. This is a frightening but all too real prospect. At present, I understand the government is not even contemplating such a law, while there are at least twenty unofficial newspapers and journals being printed in the USSR. In most cases, the quality of the paper and print is terrible, and the texts are full of typographical errors. Yet these are real, although fragile, buds of freedom which are beginning to appear under the influence of *glasnost*. With the written word bound so long in Russia, such small steps toward unleashing its power are indeed large leaps toward greater freedoms.

The Word Proclaimed: Moscow Baptist Church

We had no official plans with "Intourist" to visit any churches in the Soviet Union, but we decided to take every opportunity we could to meet Russian Christians in their own churches. Thus in the evening, our group went to the Baptist church in Moscow. It took much lengthy negotiation with the "Intourist" people before we could do so, and they were obviously not enamored of our plan, claiming that there was no bus available. We suggested that the bus that was supposed to take us to a museum should take us to the church instead. They could not really refuse, so they had to agree to our proposal, but their lack of enthusiasm was clearly apparent.

The Baptist church in Moscow is the only Protestant house of worship in a city with a population exceeding 8 million.[2] Therefore, when our bus drew up beside it, we were surrounded by hundreds of people. The congregation of this church numbers more than 5,000. It is a fine church, and has been visited by many famous preachers from Europe and America.

We were met by the well-known senior pastor of the church, Vasili Efimovich Logvinenko, who is also the chairman of the official (that is, government-approved) All-Union Council of Evangelical Christian-Baptists, which is the umbrella organization for all the Protestant denominations in the Soviet Union. I had never met Logvinenko before, but we were able to converse immediately as though we had known each other for many years.

Suddenly Pastor Logvinenko said to me, "Mikhail, how long do you need to preach? Would an hour be enough?"

That really shook me. I had not contemplated preaching during my stay in the Soviet Union. I had come to look and listen, and I said as much to Logvinenko. He laughed. "My dear Mikhail Morgulis, as soon as I mention your name, you

---

[2]During Stalin's reign all Protestant churches were incorporated into one organization for control purposes. This group, the All-Union Council of Evangelical Christians-Baptists continues today. Thus, wherever the term Baptist is used regarding a church, the reference is not to a specific denomination. Rather, all Protestant churches in the Soviet Union are called Baptist.

will have no hope of getting away without speaking. Have you forgotten our customs?"

Dear Pastor, I thought, how could I know your church rules and customs? I had never so much as set foot across the threshold of a Protestant church when I lived here. This is my first visit to an evangelical house of prayer on Russian soil. I am aware that many people listen to my weekly radio programs, watch my sermon videos, and read my articles and forewords to Christian books. They do not realize that my faith was formed and forged in the West. I knew about the historical Christ when I left Russia, but I did not know Jesus personally nor understand God's plan concerning mankind. But there was no time to say all this to Logvinenko, so I simply asked for an empty room to gather my thoughts for a few minutes.

When I was alone, I prayed: "Lord, You know that I have not prepared myself to serve You through the spoken word in Russia. Probably, in all the years of my service to You, this will be the greatest spiritual test I have ever faced. Endow me with Your wisdom and guide my tongue to the words I should say to these people, my countrymen. Amen!"

I knew that my radio programs were known to many because I receive hundreds of letters from the Soviet Union. Nevertheless, I was both surprised and uplifted to hear the loud murmur that ran around the church when Pastor Logvinenko introduced me. I began with words which came to my lips somewhat unexpectedly, but by their own volition:

Do not believe those who may say to you that Christians in America don't think about you, that they've forgotten you. Even if the most famous person in your country says so—still don't believe it! We never forget you. Of course, my words may not count for much, but they are affirmed by the authority of the Bible, the Word of God, which tells us that the church is the body of Christ. Therefore we, who believe, are parts of that body. And if some part of the body is stricken, then the whole body feels the pain. So if you are pained in Moscow, then we, in Chicago, share your pain, as you share ours. For although we believers live in different countries, we are united in the one body of Christ. If our faith is true, then when you in Russia are afflicted, we, in America, are afflicted too. If our hearts ache in America, then your hearts will echo our heartache here in Russia—if you are truly faithful. And if we pray for you, then the Lord will help you, as He will help us through the intercession of your prayers!

I went on to speak of the sufferings which are to be found all over the world, under all kinds of systems. I proposed that if we do not forget the sufferings of Christ, then our own sufferings take on a new dimension. We are often challenged: why should you believers be better than nonbelievers? Does your God spare you from suffering; do you feel pain any less than we do? No. We suffer just as much, and our pain is sometimes even greater, but we believers know why we are suffering. We know that our suffering is a reflection of the sufferings of our Lord. When we come to understand this, our sufferings acquire a new meaning—for we know why we suffer and for whom.

I then reminded them that in exchange for suffering, Christ gives us life. In other words, in coming to Christ, we are gifted with eternal life. I cited the Gospel of St. John 1:5, "The light shineth in the darkness; and the darkness comprehended it not." In conclusion, I said that our faith is put to the test every day of our lives because the battle between God and Satan goes on every day in our hearts. And finally, I called on them to pray, especially for those whose hearts have fallen to the power of the Evil One.

The Spirit Moves

For the first time in my life I saw several thousand people, both old and young, crying at once. Among them was my own sixteen-year-old daughter, who was a member of our group. She has an excellent knowledge of Russian, and understood every word. I have never seen her shed a tear in an American church, but she was crying with everyone else. As the pastor called the congregation to repentance, the wings of the Holy

Spirit could be felt in the church. Several people came forward and, with the words "Christ, my Lord," fell to their knees. I prayed with many of them, and in those moments the intensity of other people's griefs and misfortunes drew them closer to me.

The service finally came to an end, but my daughter and I could not get away. People came up to embrace us and gave us notes requesting Christian literature and cassettes. We handed out everything that we had brought with us. Seeing the joy in the recipients to whom we gave Bibles and cassettes, I found myself rejoicing in God's providence: "Thank You, Lord, thank You for being beside us at the airport customs."

As we exited from the crowds, a young scientist, Vyacheslav T., a regular listener of my religious programs, was waiting for us at the door of the pastor's study. This educated, intelligent young man stood out among others because he has been blind from birth. Yet despite this handicap, he has learned to type, and I had received many wonderful letters from him. But now, for the first time, we were meeting apart from the radio. He extended a careful hand and ran it lightly over my face.

"Everyone can see what you look like except me," said Vyacheslav. "I have listened to Western religious programs for many years," he continued. "I don't know what I'd do without them. When you spoke of suffering today, I felt as though you were speaking directly to me. I know that you were addressing everyone, of course, but our hearts are like an instrument attuned to receiving everything individually."

I had brought a shortwave receiver with a cassette tape recorder especially for him. When I put it into his hands, Vyacheslav's voice broke, "Maybe some would find this hard to believe, but I think God heard my prayer. My old radio finally broke down two days ago, and for me a radio means contact with the rest of the world. I praise God for your generosity."

After this last encounter, some of the believers accompanied us to our hotel. Everyone had something to say, questions to ask, and many had requests for prayer. Some asked for prayer for their unbelieving children, parents, or friends. Not surprisingly, dawn was already breaking when I finally climbed into my bed.

CHAPTER FOUR

Moscow Continued:
Missions, Mothers, and Markets

In the land of your birth you may
understand the song of the birds.
(Russian proverb)

August 5, 1988 . . .

Before leaving for Georgia, I was to have an extraordinary
meeting with one of the most famous personalities in Russia,
the acclaimed poet Bella Akhmadulina. Her poems are known
by heart by millions of Russian people. For that matter, translations of her poems can be found in any good American library
or university collection. Her work has already passed into the
annals of classical Russian poetry, and she is widely considered
to have inherited the mantle of two tragic Russian women of
inarguable genius—the poets Anna Akhmatova and Marina
Tsvetayeva. European journalists have dubbed Bella Akhmadulina with the title "queen of Russian poetry."

Bella lives in a block of flats on a tree-lined Moscow street.
The entrance is covered with messages from her fans: "Bella,
your poems help us to live," "Bella, we love you."

The Party of Parties
Sounds of Tchaikovsky being played on the piano filled Akhmadulina's flat, like the delicate patter of spring rain. Our fifty-
year-old hostess has wise, slanting eyes, eyes that have seen
much. As Osip Mandelstam, the poet whose death in the
camps lies at Stalin's door once said, "Poets are taken more
seriously in Russia than anywhere else; here they are killed
because of their poems."

As I looked around the room, there were other guests there already—well-known writers, cinema directors, journalists, and scientists. All of them were liberals, who support Gorbachev's policies. In general, the Russian intelligentsia is Gorbachev's main base of support. The people as a whole do not have any faith in Gorbachev's reforms, feel no personal sympathy toward him, and have no particular desire to "restructure" themselves. The "new thinking" proclaimed by Gorbachev cuts no ice with them, and this is understandable. It is hard to jettison, in a few short years, that which has been forcefully inculcated into your parents, and then into you, for some seventy years.

I realized that many of the guests at this party were part of the Soviet elite. In fact, one of Gorbachev's "shadow cabinets" is the Cultural Fund, which includes prominent scientists, writers, and for that matter, Gorbachev's wife, Raisa. My hostess, Bella Akhmadulina, is also a member of this Fund, and is on friendly terms with the Soviet Union's First Lady.

On the initiative of the members of the Cultural Fund, careful feelers have been put out concerning the need to publish the Bible in the Soviet Union and to ensure its legal import from abroad. Recent events have shown that certain gains have already been made in this sphere. Regulations have been adopted stipulating the right to bring Bibles into the Soviet Union and send them by post. For instance, in 1988 alone, my organization, the Slavic Gospel Association, sent more than 250,000 Bibles to the USSR.[1]

Behind Every Great Man Is a Great Mother

While at Bella's party, I took the opportunity to follow up on a rumor that I had heard. I asked one of the guests whether it was true that Gorbachev's mother was a religious believer.

"Yes," he replied. "She lives in the Stavropol region, in the village of Razdolnoye. She is a regular churchgoer, not just on

---

[1]From time to time, there are sensational claims in the Western press that this or that organization has managed to get a million Bibles into the Soviet Union. Those who have not actually engaged in this kind of work can easily claim any number of books. In actual fact, it is a serious problem to get in as many as 100 Bibles.

Sundays. People say she comes to church on weekdays, and even more frequently of late. She prays for long periods of time. Everyone knows who she prays for."

There is a custom in Russian Orthodox churches whereby parishioners write down the names of those for whom they ask intercession, and it is passed to the priest for prayer for those particular people. It is said that lately Orthodox priests have been receiving thousands of notes, asking them to pray for "Mikhail." Obviously they do not mean Mikhail Baryshnikov or Mikhail Morgulis. This is another evidence, I believe, of the Spirit's moving in Russia.

Before leaving the party, I gave Bibles to some of the other guests. One of them, a very prominent writer, ran his hand gently over the cover of the Bible and said quietly to me, "Russia needs this much more than any number of blue jeans."

A New Word Heard: Christian Publishing

There was another exceptional meeting waiting for us in Moscow. One of the largest Soviet publishing houses, *Znaniye* (Knowledge) had approached the American firm Victor Books (Scripture Press Publications, Inc.) for translation and publication rights for one of their books—*How to Really Love Your Child*—by American psychologist Dr. Ross Campbell.

There were certain important questions to be resolved, and Victor Books had asked me to represent them on this mission in Moscow, a request I was delighted to accept. Interestingly enough, my discussion and subsequent correspondence with the Soviet publishers was quite contentious. For instance, they wanted to include a condition in the contract allowing them to shorten the translation at their own discretion. I realized at once that this would mean that all the Christian content would be excised, and so I flatly refused their request. Furthermore, I insisted that the contract stipulate that I would be sent a copy of the completed translation for review before it went to the printers. The Soviet publishers were highly indignant about my demands, and wanted financial concessions in return. I accused them of unfair practices, but agreed to their terms. Two months later they sent a letter agreeing to the conditions of our contract. For Russia, this is indeed an event of historic significance, for this is the first time in the past seventy years that a Soviet publisher is printing an American Christian book. The print run is an amazing 500,000 copies!

There are a number of things I should clarify in this connection. Before Gorbachev the Reformer nailed his slogans to the sagging walls of the edifice of the Soviet state, no serious works on child rearing were published in the USSR. All that was available were propaganda-inspired, pseudoscientific treatises, which were of no practical use to parents. Of foreign authors, the only one to be published was Dr. Benjamin Spock, whose theories on child rearing were considered acceptable because of his leftist sympathies. In the meantime, Spock has revised many of his "early" ideas on child care. But in the Soviet Union, Dr. Spock is reprinted from time to time, with forewords hailing his book as "the newest achievement" in the psychology of raising children.

The "generation gap" problem is shaking the foundations of the whole world, and in Russia, nowadays, it has become more acute than ever before. Thus, the state is looking for solutions to this problem in various ways: through sociological studies, culture analysis, and now finally Western family practice works. In my own view, which I believe to be the biblical one, the problem of "fathers and sons" will continue as long as humanity exists. However, "fathers" will always search for some medicine that will at least lessen the pain, even if it cannot completely heal the wound.

For this reason, the previously mentioned Cultural Fund is encouraging Soviet publishing houses to search out suitable literature from the lists of foreign publishers. (Regardless of what some argue, it is indisputable that in some matters the interests of Christians and Communists coincide fully.) Hence the choice of the Campbell book.

Of course, American readers see nothing strange about a Christian book being translated into another language. But Russian readers, believers and nonbelievers alike, were amazed by this occurrence. They realized that even with a print run of half a million copies, the book will be virtually unobtainable. I even received advance requests from people anxious to acquire a copy. They were right about the demand. The Soviet official responsible for the distribution of the book, knowing his market, told me that all 500,000 copies would be sold out in three days.

The Electric House Church

On my last day in Moscow, I managed to squeeze in a visit to a small house church, whose members are regular listeners to my radio program. There were about fourteen people there, all of them middle-aged. They were studying the Bible according to a plan they have worked out by themselves. They had a number of Russian language books published by our Slavic Gospel Press: Josh McDowell's *Evidence That Demands a Verdict,* C.S. Lewis' *Mere Christianity,* Billy Graham's *Approaching Hoofbeats,* and works by F.F. Bruce, Francis Schaeffer, and others.

They have a video cassette recorder (VCR), but the range of Russian language videos at their disposal is a narrow one, although they have some Moody Science films and the popular *Jesus* film. They told me how vital it is for them to get some video recordings of really serious, profound sermons.

VCRs have been manufactured in the Soviet Union for some years now, but they are of very poor quality, and the prices charged for them are astronomical—1200–1500 rubles. To buy a foreign-made VCR takes 2500–2800 rubles. Remember these prices in light of the average monthly salary in the Soviet Union of 120–180 rubles.

Recently, churches have been pooling their resources to buy a good quality foreign VCR for common use, enabling them to show Christian films in the individual churches. Earlier this would have been impossible because of the need to get permission from the authorities. Moreover, in the past, many older believers were offended by the very idea of "films."

An Unexpected Visitor

But let us return to the little house church. Its members try to bring along new people every Saturday. They show them films, read extracts from books and the Bible to them, discuss religious questions, and pray. On the day I visited them they had a newcomer, a tall, nervous young girl. Her hair was combed back in the traditional Russian manner, she had a clear, high forehead, but extraordinarily burning blue eyes. I was told that she was a nonbeliever, who had recently been deserted by the man with whom she was in love. A week earlier she had tried to commit suicide, but she was intercepted, and brought here. At present, they told me, she was staying at the house church. Not long after meeting her, the girl asked if she could have a private word with me. We went out into the kitchen. Her name was a beautiful, old one—Varya.

She looked piercingly into my eyes and asked, "Do believers feel pain less than nonbelievers? Is everything different for you?"

I repeated to her what I had said in the Moscow Baptist church, "If only that were the case, Varya. But no, we feel just as much pain as anybody else. But knowing the sufferings through which Christ went—and why He did so—gives our pain a different meaning. We know why we suffer, and for whom we suffer. A believer's sufferings mirror the sufferings of our Lord. That is what puts a different complexion on our pain. But our tears are just as salty as those of anybody else, if not more so."

I left this group not knowing Varya's fate. But a week later I telephoned the house church from another city, and was overjoyed to hear the glad tidings that Varya had accepted Christ.

You Never Know Who Is Listening

Riding back from the house church to the hotel, I fell into conversation with the taxi driver who had brought me, a fair-haired man of about thirty-five.

"Every evening when I get home," he told me, "my two kids ask me about the passengers I've had that day. Was there anyone interesting? Tell me, who are you?"

"Tell your children that one of your passengers today was a servant. No, don't look at me like that: I really am a servant—

a servant of God, and I am glad to be so. My main occupation is publishing books. I also do a little writing myself and some radio work, but my most important function is being a servant."

He seemed stunned, sat there biting his lips as if recalling something, and then responded, "You said that you appear on the radio. I thought your voice sounded familiar. Would you mind telling me your name—if that's not a state secret?"

I told him my name, and he almost crashed into another car.

"What do you know, I often listen to your broadcasts on Sunday! Would you mind if we dropped by my place for a moment, so that my kids could take a look at you? Please, just for a minute."

I felt I had no right to refuse such a request, so we stopped by at his home. But as bad luck would have it, the children had gone out. My driver almost wept with frustration.

"Never mind," I comforted him, "I'll leave you an illustrated children's Bible. That will be more important to them than seeing me."

"How much is the Bible?"

"Not a penny. I brought such books to give to people free of charge. Tell your children that it is a present for them from American Christians."

As we drove off for the hotel, he suddenly said, as if in answer to some thought he had been turning over in his mind, "If everyone wanted to be a servant rather than a master, how good life would be."

I could only think to myself, how true, my fast friend. Indeed, is this not the simple message that our Lord was trying to teach? How often it falls on deaf ears in Russia as well as in America.

CHAPTER FIVE

The Gospel in Georgia

When you get to the top of the
mountain, look around you and not
under your feet.
(Georgian saying)

August 5–7, 1988 . . .

Farewell, Moscow! We set off for Tbilisi, the capital of Georgia in the Caucasus, the birthplace of one of the greatest tyrants of all time—Stalin. Tbilisi is a fascinating city. Geographically it lies in the subtropics, so there is a multitude of fruit such as mandarins, grapes, and melons. The city is surrounded by picturesque mountains, whose peaks reach into the clouds.

Impressions of Georgia

The Georgians are an ancient people, who have lived in the mountains of the Caucasus for thousands of years. Their language and culture bears no relation whatsoever to Russian language and culture. These mountain people are brave and possess a fiery temperament. Traditionally Christian, the Georgians were resolute in beating back attacks by Turkish Muslims. Although there have been many wonderful Georgian writers and artists, they also gave the world Joseph Stalin and his henchman Lavrenti Beria, the monstrous butcher who headed the KGB.

Incidentally, the current Soviet minister of Foreign Affairs, the liberal and affable Shevardnadze, also hails from these parts. The Georgians, whose pride is a byword, complained to me that when then President Reagan visited the Soviet

Union, he was supposed to come to Georgia too, but cancelled at the last moment. The local feeling was that their fellow countryman Shevardnadze had not been sufficiently pressing in inviting Reagan to the Georgian republic.

"Our President is not a young man," I replied, seeking to soften the blow. "It's likely that his doctors advised him from going into the mountains."

They clicked their tongues in exasperation and responded: "What nonsense! Being in the mountains is very healthy. Our people are world-renowned for longevity!"

It is true that life expectancy here is very high, especially in the region of Abkhazia. My readers may well remember an American television advertisement showing a 100-year-old Abkhazian in a huge hat advertising yogurt as a means of prolonging one's lifespan. It would be interesting to find out just how much truth lies behind this claim.

After a daytime visit to the museum of Georgian art, I was invited to take part in a discussion on Georgian culture. Although I do not consider myself to be an expert in this highly specialized field, I did venture a number of opinions.

Among other things, I expressed profound appreciation of the great Georgian poet Shota Rustaveli, the author of the poem "Warrior in a Tigerskin": this work is one of the greatest treasures of ancient human culture. Then I noted that one of my favorite artists is their countryman, Pirosmani. This amazing artist managed to combine in his work the simplicity of a child with the wisdom of a sage. He wandered around Georgia drawing immortal pictures on the oilcloth covers of restaurants in exchange for a meal. Nowadays these pictures are exhibited in the greatest galleries of the world, and are priced at hundreds of thousands of dollars.

With sadness and affection I also recalled two marvelous contemporary Georgian poets, Titsian Tabidze and Pado Yashvili, who were killed on the orders of Stalin and Beria. Finally I said that although Christianity had had an immense influence on Georgian culture and raised it to incredible heights, how wonderful it would be if every person today were to confront the claims of Christ on an individual level.

Taxi Testimony: A Surprise Encounter

That evening we were expected in a church in Tbilisi, with a congregation of some 5,000–6,000 people of various nationalities. For this reason, the services are held in four languages: Georgian, Russian, Armenian, and Ossetian. Each language group gathers at different times, but to meet us, all of them came together on the one occasion.

The church could not hold more than 2,000 people, so it was impossible for everyone to get inside. The problem was solved by putting additional loudspeakers outside, and there was a large crowd around the church right throughout the meeting.

I made my way to the church separately from the rest of the group, and again the Lord gifted me with a surprising encounter. The driver of the taxi which I caught was a man of about forty-eight, but fatigue and worry made him seem much older. When I told him my destination, his face brightened suddenly and, after a moment's pause, he confided, "I know that place. My mother used to go there."

"Maybe she will be there today?" I replied.

"No. She died three years ago."

"And have you ever been to church?"

"No, I don't think that's for me."

"But what do you think your mother did in church?"

"Prayed, I guess."

"For whom?"

"How should I know? I suppose anyone can pray for anyone."

"I'm sure that most of her prayers would have been for you."

"What makes you say that?"

"Because all mothers the world over pray for their children, for their happiness. . . . And, of course, every believing mother wants her children to come to know God."

"I only used to drive her there, but never went inside. She left me two books—a Bible and a Christian hymnbook. They're still on a small table, just where they always lay while she was alive. I've never looked into them, though."

"May I venture a small suggestion? Open them. Maybe they will explain what your mother prayed for."

Return to the Tower of Babel

After still another surprise encounter, I had an even greater sense of being on God's mission in the Soviet Union.

Before the meeting, as is the custom in all evangelical churches in Russia, we knelt with the pastors and deacons to ask God to bless today's gathering. For some reason, as we prayed, I had a mental vision of the stony road to Golgotha, along which Christ walked to fulfill the will of the Father. I remembered accounts of how He fell to His knees under the weight of the cross. To this day Russian believers preserve the tradition of showing reverence by kneeling when addressing themselves to God.

Eventually the service began. At first, I acted as interpreter for two American pastors from our group: the well-known radio evangelist Dan Bruce, representing Presbyterian churches, and Marvin Hoogland of the Christian Reformed churches. In fact, the whole thing was reminiscent of a mini Tower of Babel, because I would translate from English into Russian, and my words, in turn, were further translated into Georgian, while within the body of the hall, difficult bits were being translated into Armenian and Ossetian.

Then I was asked to take the service. I looked at the people sitting before me. As is the custom, women were seated separately. The front rows were occupied by older people, with the younger ones further back. Before the meeting I was told that a lot of believers had come from other towns. It was very hot and stuffy, but the Holy Spirit brought His peace to this church nonetheless.

As I began to speak it seemed as if I was watching myself from a place beyond my body. The words which came from my lips were like burning coals which had seared me. Judging by the reactions of the people, the Lord had again prompted me with the right words to say in this particular gathering. I spoke again of sufferings, that the most painful of them are those which believers inflict on one another. I recalled the words of

John, the apostle of love: "If a man say, I love God, and hateth his brother, he is a liar: for he that loveth not his brother whom he hath seen, how can he love God whom he hath not seen?" (1 John 4:20)

On this occasion too there were many tears and repentances. Quite unexpectedly, my eye fell upon the taxi driver who had brought me to the church. He was standing just inside the door. And the words of St. Paul to his favorite disciple Timothy flashed into my mind: "When I call to remembrance the unfeigned faith that is in thee, which dwelt first in thy grandmother Lois, and thy mother Eunice; and I am persuaded that in thee also" (2 Timothy 1:5).

With difficulty, the driver managed to work his way forward, and finally reaching me, sank to his knees.

I simply said to him, "Let us pray together to God, to whom your mother prayed, and in her memory." I sensed the Spirit working in his life.

When the service was over, nobody dispersed, just like in Moscow. Questions, questions, and more questions—I was led aside by a group of young men and girls.

"We've all come from other towns," they explained. "We want to talk to you separately." So we agreed to an evening meeting.

Questions, Questions, Questions

We gathered in a park near my hotel. There were about twenty of them, all in their early twenties, including four young men currently serving in the Soviet army, but dressed in civilian clothes. It was they who asked the first questions, concerning any possible compromises permitted in the Bible regarding believers serving military duty.

I replied that the Bible does not allow for compromises in its main spiritual tenets. If our spiritual perception is good, we can always see unfailingly what relates to God and what relates to humans. The whole world is familiar with Christ's dictum on this question, "Render to Caesar the things that are Caesar's, and to God the things that are God's" (Mark 12:17). Yes, we must obey the laws of our lands, even if we do not approve of some of them. We can disobey only a law which demands that we renounce God.

As we talked, two militiamen—the Soviet equivalent of policemen—strolled up to us, eyed us suspiciously, and asked why we had gathered here. The young folks hurried to assure them (as had been prearranged) that we were all on our way back from a birthday party and had stopped in the park to chat.

When the militiamen went away, I said to my companions, "What are you afraid of? This is a time of *glasnost,* you know that."

"We know it," they responded, "but does the militia? This isn't Moscow, you know!"

Their caution was understandable. The fruits of Gorbachev's *glasnost* and *perestroika* are really only visible in the two largest cities, Moscow and Leningrad. On the periphery, even in large towns, there is not much evidence of any winds of change. The storms of *perestroika* in Moscow and Leningrad are only barely discernible ripples away from the "center," and nothing has changed under the surface. In Georgia too there are only ripples.

CHAPTER SIX

Higher Up and Further In

So, you want to know about life.
Take off your shoes to walk more
easily.   (Georgian proverb)

August 8, 1988 . . .

The following day, a Georgian couple, both believers, caught
me outside the hotel. They had spent the whole night there,
waiting, so as not to miss us when we left. They had been
unable to enter the hotel to see me because Soviet citizens
may not, as a rule, go into hotels where foreigners stay. They
are turned away by vigilant doormen, the duty militiaman outside, or at least by the plainclothes militiaman on duty in the
hotel foyer.

The husband was a classic mountain-dweller, of enormous
height, with thick brows beetling above piercing black eyes.
The wife was a friendly, cheerful woman with kind brown
eyes, who wore the inevitable head scarf. They lived up in the
mountains, in a Georgian village some eighty miles from Tbilisi. They are the only believers in their area. He is a veterinari-
an, she is a housewife. They told us that up in the mountains a
lot of nonbelievers listen to our Christian broadcasts on Trans-
World Radio from Monte Carlo in Monaco. They knew, they
said, that by law I did not have the right to separate from our
group, but they wished that I could meet the people of their
village.

I opened my mouth to say that yes, it was unfortunate that I
could not break away from the group, but instead of that,
found myself saying, "For something like that—it's worth the

risk. My daughter and I will go with you, but we must be back tonight. See if you can find someone who can drive a car fast, and can be trusted to keep his mouth shut."

Half an hour later they were back with just such a man. And so began another adventure that God had in store for me.

A Whirlwind Pilgrimage

The road into the mountains was breathtakingly beautiful, but frequently ran right alongside a sheer drop of terrifying height. Naturally, it was an unpaved road, strewn with quite large rocks. Possibly the driver felt that driving around such rocks was an unwarranted indulgence, or maybe he thought it foolhardy to maneuver from side to side so close to the edge of the cliff. Whatever the reason, though, our dirty, yellow taxi leapt and shuddered as though it were suffering an epileptic seizure.

The taxi, actually, deserves a description all of its own. Half of the instruments didn't work, the doors would not shut completely, the trunk was tied down with a piece of rope, and every time the driver braked, the pedal went right down to the floor. We roared, rattled, and squealed along, but the driver did not seem to find anything amiss, and indeed, wore the contented expression of a rider satisfied with his steed. We, on the other hand, had the constant feeling that we were on some exciting, but hair-raising fairground ride. Nor was there much comfort to be gained from the cabby's adherence to the local custom of driving with only one hand on the steering wheel. Yet, despite everything, we continued toward our destination without any mishaps.

When the driver, a middle-aged Georgian, discovered that we were from America, he burst first out into excited, hoarse speech in Georgian, and then switched to elementary Russian, "Look here, friend! One of our ancient churches is just a few miles from here. If you don't go to see it now, you'll probably never get another chance. You don't have to pay me—I'll drive you there free of charge!"

The church turned out to be a magnificent third-century structure. Naturally, it was almost entirely in ruins. Enormous brown stones lay immobile, turned up to the sky; massive columns supported a moss-covered arch. Christian pilgrims have a custom of leaving pages of the Bible here, pages they have copied out by hand. There was a countless number of such pages, held down by small stones to stop them from being carried away by the wind. It was a fascinating testimony to the spiritual power of the Word in people's lives.

A spring of incredibly clear and delicious water gurgled in the churchyard. The taxi driver told us that people bring their children here, to give them a taste of real mountain water. Many adults believe that the spring has medicinal qualities which guard against illness. We drank long and deep of this bright, crystal-clear water and then continued on our journey.

Ministry in the Village

About two hours later we reached the mountain village. Lean black pigs roamed along its streets. Swarthy-complexioned women in dark clothing peered at us over fences. The dusty streets were lined with nut trees.

We greeted everyone in the traditional Georgian manner, *"Gamarjobo, genatsvale!"* that is—"Greetings, friend!" I knew that Georgians, especially the mountain-dwellers, are very particular about observing the proper courtesies. They hold that even a foe must be greeted politely. The men, who were working, responded in kind, putting down their hoes and tools to watch us. In such a village as this, most of the inhabitants are farmers and shepherds.

We went to the edge of the village where there was a clear and fast-flowing stream. With exquisite enjoyment, we waded into its cold, swift currents. The sky above us was a dazzling blue. It was a beautiful pastoral setting. "Praise the Lord!" I called out to my daughter at the top of my voice. A whole horde of brown-skinned Georgian children splashed and shouted around us. I called them over to me, handed out chewing gum and badges, and asked whether they all understood Russian. They nodded—after all, Russian is a compulsory subject in all Georgian schools.

A small girl, with eyes like huge, ripe plums, piped up, "I

thought Americans looked completely different."

"I bet you thought they had three ears and two noses, didn't you?" I teased her.

We also gave the children postal stickers with a white dove and the words "Jesus Loves You" on them. The little girl read these words painstakingly, and then said, "Why does He love me? He's not my daddy."

We told them about Christ, how He loved children, and how He told adults to be trusting like children. I explained that as parents we always wish to take our children's pains on ourselves whenever there is anything wrong with them. Our hearts ache for them, but there is no way we can shift their pain to ourselves. But Christ did take on everyone's sufferings, both adults and children. After this short lesson on the bank of the stream, we promised the children that we would send them copies of the Russian-language children's illustrated Bible we publish at Slavic Gospel Association.

Back in our friends' house, a whole lot of people were already waiting for us. The Georgian rules of hospitality had already come into play: tables covered with white cloths stood in the garden, bearing large dishes of huge, sweet-smelling apples, golden grapes, and ruddy-skinned oranges and mandarins.

Georgia is the only place with a subtropical climate in the Soviet Union. Huge chunks of yellow melons lay side by side with bright-red slices of watermelon. A lamb had been slaughtered in honor of the visitors from afar, and shish kebabs were being prepared.

The shepherds came down from the hills and sat apart in a group of their own for the feast. The men, looking so much alike, were almost comical with their bushy, black brows overshadowing their hooked noses.

"Remember, Mikhail, these people are nonbelievers," our host reminded me quietly.

A Not So Traditional Speech
When everybody was seated, a *tamada* (toastmaster) was elected in accordance with Georgian custom. His task is to

ensure that everything goes smoothly and to guide the order of toasts proposed, songs sung, and other impromptu amusements. Speeches play a very important role at the table in Georgia, and the fame of masterly "speechmakers" travels far and wide. They are just as admired as actors or well-known athletes. By tradition, the toastmaster offered the right of the first word to me, the guest.

Given still another opportunity to testify for Christ, I began by saying, "I believe that all our encounters are ordained from above. Therefore, I am certain that our unusual and unexpected meeting today is also by God's will. What is the reason? I don't know, but I believe that in time the Lord shall make His providential design plain to me and to you. And now, I would like to ask you to allow me to pray to the One who granted me the opportunity of standing here in your midst in your beautiful land."

I prayed for their mountains, their magnificent nation, their widows' tears, their far-from-easy life, their pride, and their children. I concluded by asking God to open their hearts to Him.

How Can I Be Forgiven?

A man in a full-length sheepskin cloak came up to me and told me that he belonged to the *Svanov* tribe, which still practices blood feud.

Officially, blood feuds are a thing of the past, but in fact they continue to exist, though not on such a widespread scale as in the past.

His Russian was strongly accented, and grammatically poor, but I understood him to say, "We live high up in the mountains so that we have less chance of meeting strangers on the road. That way our hot heads encounter less temptation. Now you tell me, will God forgive me if I've killed someone?"

I said nothing, and he continued, "We met up by chance in the mountains, and he bragged that one of his kinfolk had once killed a cousin of mine. Well, I just couldn't let that pass. I had my rifle with me and managed to shoot before he did. The authorities concluded that he had fallen to his death over a cliff.

That was twelve years ago. So, tell me, will God forgive me or not?"

I looked him straight in the eye and responded, "As I see you now before me—no, He won't."

His nostrils quivered, and his eyes flashed fire. He retorted, "But you said on the radio that God forgives everyone. Did you lie?"

"No, I didn't lie. And now, you tell me, to whom did you come today to ask that question? Well, tell me!"

"Why, to you."

"To me, a mere mortal, like yourself. But God says that He will forgive those who come to Him. So you must come to Him, and He will give you your answer."

"How do you know that? How do you know what God wills?"

"Of course I don't completely, but I do know the words of God, recorded in His book, the Bible. Let's look at them together."

I opened the Bible and found all the passages I could remember about forgiveness. He hunched over the Bible like a huge, black bird of prey.

"Do you have one in Georgian?"

"Not with me, unfortunately."

"All right then, leave me the Russian one. I'll give you three sheep in exchange or five if you want."

I couldn't help laughing. "My friend, they won't let me aboard a plane with five sheep! You keep them. And keep this Bible too. It is free, like God's forgiveness."

How Can a Man Be Born When He Is Old?

Our host introduced me to the oldest of the shepherds, a man who was 103 years old. The old man looked at me sharply, his eyes bright as a bird's.

"I don't read books," he told me. "I only listen to the radio, Georgian broadcasts from the West. I sometimes listen to you too. You keep insisting that faith will save people. Well, we all believe in God, we're all Christians. So that means we're saved."

"How many children have you got?" I asked him.

"Six sons, one daughter, fourteen grandchildren, thirty-four great-grandchildren, and there are a few more, besides—I can't recall offhand."

"Do they say that they love you?"

"Of course."

"And how many of them, do you think, really love you?"

"Who can say?"

"Well, the same applies to God. We all claim to love Him and believe in Him. But how many of us really trust everything to Him?"

I could sense that I was not getting through to him. My mind raced around for another example to make myself clear. Georgian folklore abounds with parables. This biblical form of storytelling usually leaves an impression on its listeners. The Lord brought to mind a story which was very apt for this particular occasion, and I recounted it to the old man:

A man who believed in God was walking along a mountain trail at the very edge of a steep drop. Suddenly he stumbled and toppled over into the precipice. But at the last moment he managed to catch hold of a tree growing at its very edge, and hung there, above the chasm. He cried out: "Lord, please help me, for I am a believer!" And the Lord heard his plea, and said to the man: "I will help you, but first tell Me, do you truly believe in Me?"

"Of course I believe in You truly, but please, Lord, help me!"

"In a moment. But first tell Me again: do you truly and completely believe in Me?"

"In everything! Always! Save me, Lord!"

"Yes, one more second. Tell me for the last time: Do you have absolute faith in Me?"

"Absolutely! Absolutely in everything, Lord!"

"Then listen to what I tell you: if you truly believe in Me, let go of that tree."

The gnarled hands of the old man were clenched tightly around his staff; he watched me in silence. Everyone else was silent too, listening to the parable.

I sighed. "Absolute faith is when we can let go of the tree."

The old man shook his head. "What about you? Do you think that *you* would have been able to let go, eh?"

"I don't know, maybe not; it's very hard. I often pray that should such a time come, I will be able to let go."

Later, as we prepared to depart, we left two shortwave radios and various other gifts. Our host came up to me and revealed, "They wouldn't talk on this subject before. Now they'll repeat that parable."

Once again, the Lord had been faithful in helping to plant a seed for His kingdom.

Finally, it was our turn to be showered with presents. My daughter and I received a long deer horn for drinking wine, an ancient dagger, a traditional Georgian white felt hat, and the most impressive present of all—a long, thick shepherd's cloak woven out of goat's hair. These cloaks are so thick and warm, that shepherds wearing them can comfortably sleep on the ground on cold mountain nights.

Along with the cloak we received a message. "This is for your kind words, and in memory of Georgia," said the old shepherd. "Don't forget us."

I was certain that I would not.

There and Back Again

We traveled back through pitch darkness. The taxi's motor roared and strained as we labored up steep grades and then plunged down again, never knowing whether we were still on the road or hurtling into a precipice. My daughter and I clasped hands and prayed in between answering the driver's questions about America. I was so pleased on this occasion, and in future tense situations, that my sixteen-year-old daughter behaved so maturely.

As everywhere in the Soviet Union, there have been some changes in Georgia over the past ten years. There are more attractive tall buildings; old monuments are being restored. There is a great deal more free expression in the press. Not to the same degree as in Moscow, but progressively more as time goes by. However, those who know Georgia well would notice that not all the changes have been for the better. Georgia used to have one of the highest living standards of all the Soviet republics. The people here knew how to make money and at the same time help one another. There were unofficial enterprises (so-called brigades) manufacturing items out of wool. Many made money on trading in the fruits of the region, selling them in other Soviet cities. However, in recent years, special militia groups charged with stamping out "economic violations" have wiped out just about every means of supplementary income in Georgia. Therefore, daily life in the cities has become much harder, there is little worth buying in the shops, and the prices at the markets have rocketed. Traditional Georgian hospitality has remained unchanged, but there's not much that one can offer one's guests. Bearing in mind the specifics of the Georgian national character, this is a sad circumstance which contributes to major psychological stress.

God Is Lord Over All Regimes
Dramatic changes have taken place in Georgian society. The people in the street have lost their old, carefree look. And this sometimes leads to totally unpredictable, startling results. I had occasion to speak to an elderly man, who was an ordinary worker, and asked how he was finding life. "Life was easier for us ordinary people under Stalin," he answered unequivocally.

I was thunderstruck. "What on earth are you saying? I mean, I know he was a countryman of yours, but he was a murderer. And he didn't spare his own people either. I believe he had something like a quarter of a million Georgians killed."

"I don't know about that," he retorted doggedly. "Maybe there were some that he killed, but things were easier for us common folk. We always had plenty of food and never had to worry about feeding our families properly. Now that's all we can think about—how to "get" everything. It's not enough just to have money these days, but you've got to find people who won't be scared of you and who'll sell you goods and food without charging three times more than what they're worth. Gorbachev has made everyone scared. People are frightened of each other. There's no trust. No, things were much better under Stalin."

"Was anyone repressed in your family under Stalin?" I persisted.

"My wife's brother was," he admitted reluctantly, "but I never really knew him all that well."

The ancient Romans weren't being lyrical, but practical, I thought, with their motto of "bread and circuses": there's always a demand for that, through all the ages. They had a clear vision of the fallibility of human nature.

"Panem et circensis!"—is that not the cry today too? Only just bread is no longer enough. Give us delicacies, and not just circuses, but spectacles to make our blood freeze. There are no gladiators, but there are sportsmen and actors to take their place. And the roar of the crowd all too often drowns out Christ's directive to strive toward the highest.

Yet I realize God finds His children even here. Maybe it takes longer than in other parts of Russia, but the Georgians are turning their faces toward the living Christ. No matter what party is in control of the political system, God's Spirit is working in every nation throughout history to bring about His divine, sovereign plan.

CHAPTER SEVEN

An Armenian Addendum

God, spare me from my friends,
and I'll deliver myself from my
enemies.   (Russian saying)

August 8, 1988 . . .

Although I was not able to travel to Armenia during this trip, I did have a significant encounter with some Armenians. Before I describe that meeting, however, I must make a brief digression to make some points about Armenia. The Armenians are one of the most ancient nations on earth. They are mentioned in the Bible as the inhabitants of the kingdom of Urartu (Ararat). Historians and theologians have agreed that after the Flood, Noah's ark came to rest on the famous Mount Ararat.

The Armenians are predominantly Christian and belong to the Gregorian branch of the Orthodox Church. This wise, ancient nation has an immensely rich culture, but a very tragic history. For centuries they were under severe persecution from the Turks who slew and tortured countless Armenians in an effort to force them to convert to Islam. Yet the small Armenian nation did not break. It remained true to its faith and drank from the cup of suffering and sorrows with courage to the bitter end. Suffice to say that in 1914 the Turks slew 1.5 million Armenians in the first genocide of the 20th century. Armenia became part of the USSR in 1923. But in this time of *perestroika,* new sufferings have befallen the Armenians.

On one side, Armenia's neighbor is Christian Georgia, on the other—Muslim Azerbaijan. At one stage, the Soviet government incorporated a small Armenian region—Nagorny Ka-rabakh—into Azerbaijan. The rationale behind this transfer is extremely questionable. At the time it did not seem very important, but nowadays it has become the cause of atrocities and deaths. The Armenians, who make up 80 percent of the population of Nagorny Karabakh, recently demanded to be re-incorporated into Armenia. It started with a few slogans, and ended in a bloodbath and pogroms (organized massacres) mounted against the Armenians by the Muslim Azeris. Soviet officials sent from Moscow are currently conducting investigations against bandits and violators, but are refusing to rejoin Karabakh to Armenia.

Their reasoning is obvious: if they were to allow at least one change of internal borders within the *multinational* Soviet empire, demands would come flooding in from all over the place, for instance, from the Ukrainians, from the Belorussians, from the Moldavians, and from the Baltic states—all of whom have suppressed but smoldering territorial pretensions. The real question is what kind of an example would that be to "fraternal socialist countries" who might also start nourishing such unhealthy ideas. The fat would really be in the fire then! As a matter of fact, the Baltic states and the Moldavians, undeterred by the failure of the "premiere" in Armenia, also began to stage demonstrations to demand restitution of their borders. They met without success, though. The Soviet government talks glibly about all sorts of liberties, but is unwilling to run risks in chancy situations.

The brutal slaughter of the Armenians came as a severe shock to the intelligentsia in the Soviet Union. Everyone had been certain that after seventy years of Soviet power and after seventy years of talk about friendship between nations in the USSR, such a thing could not possibly happen. Especially shocking was the knowledge that the authorities in Azerbaijan did nothing to defend the Armenians, but supported the murderers, bandits, and marauders. This exposed, once and for all, the myth that the Soviet regime had brought about amity between ethnic groups.

I remember how, twenty years ago, I traveled through Soviet Central Asia, where there are some 65 million Soviet Muslims. It was there that I encountered an unexpected tendency among the locals. It was best expressed by one Kazakh, whose tongue became loosened by vodka—"You're white, and we're yellow," he said. "You just wait; the Chinese will come and drive you out!"

The malevolent breath of universally advancing Islam is felt in the Muslim areas of the Soviet Union too. The late Ayatollah Khomeini's rantings and those of Colonel Mohammar Qadaffi strike a sympathetic chord in the hearts of many "Soviet" Muslims. It is no secret in today's world that Christianity and Judaism are on the defensive, while Islam, so long dormant, is gathering strength and aspiring to the whole world.

The Curse of Cain Continues

I was alerted to the Armenian situation one morning as I was climbing aboard the bus to return to Tbilisi. I was stopped by several young men. One of them, with enormous burning eyes, explained, "We're Armenians. We've just come from our capital, Yerevan, to see you. You know that no foreigners are being allowed into Armenia at the moment. But we want you to tell Americans when you get back home what our people have just had to go through in Nagorny Karabakh."

I said to the young Armenians that I could not hold up the bus, but if they came to the airport, there would be about half an hour during which we could talk. They jumped into their car and followed our bus.

At the airport, we resumed our conversation. They explained, "The authorities are concealing the fact that pogroms took place not only in Karabakh, but in other cities as well. Hundreds of people died. Here's a list—and it's by no means a full one—of casualties, with the addresses of the dead, a description of what happened, and the findings of the postmortems."

This incomplete list contained the names of sixty people. Reading the postmortems made my hair stand on end. People had been doused with gasoline and set on fire. Women were brutally raped and had their breasts hacked off. Babies were knifed and had their eyes gouged out. It all seemed so hideously unreal under the bright blue skies above the airport.

"Is all this really true?" I asked incredulously.

The Armenians cast their hands up in dismay. "It's only a small fraction of what happened. Don't forget that those papers you are holding are the official postmortem findings."

"The terrifying thing is," whispered one of them, "that people, who one day greeted each other politely in the street and knew each other for years, suddenly turned into vicious killers. That means that it was just under the surface, it could have broken free at any moment. Of what note now is the fact that we were all members of the same trade unions and other Soviet organizations—that the newspapers wrote glowingly about our friendship? It was a sham, no more. Such flimsy pretense collapsed under the pressure of national hatred."

I didn't know what to say, even what to ask. Of course, I had read about all these events, about the deaths, but this was my first encounter with living witnesses of these terrible, pathological brutalities.

Interrupting one another, the Armenians went on: "We want the whole world to know the truth about what really happened. We have endured much as a nation throughout our entire history, and we shall survive this too. But the world must know that there is no such thing as brotherhood of nations in the Soviet Union. In fact, many of the nationalities actively hate each other. No government, no slogans, and no appeals can force people to love one another."

I was stunned by their revelations and promised to tell the truth about their plight when I returned to the West. I couldn't help but wonder, how far indeed have we come since Cain's slaying of that first brother.

Reflections in Flight

Sitting in the plane later on the way to Yalta, I realized that it is true that love cannot be enforced by governments. Love with the power to overcome national bigotries can come only through Jesus Christ.

I thought about my friends—Armenians, poets, translators,

artists. If they were to ask me now: "Why does God allow such things to happen?" I would be hard-pressed to find an answer for them.

Recently, when Armenia was devastated by a dreadful earthquake, I thought about this again. It is probable that a lot of believers, if they were to be asked who has earned the wrath of God, would reply, "The Muslims, of course, for they killed and violated the Commandments of Christ and God." Yet the earthquake struck Armenia, not Azerbaijan! And it would seem that an injustice took place. The innocents, who had already suffered, had to suffer again.

But this only serves to remind us, once more, that the life of our planet unfolds in accordance with divine providence. The ways of God are beyond the knowledge of men. Our perception of divine justice and the absolute justice of God can often seem to be in contradiction, for His ways are not ours and are beyond the grasp of our mortal understanding.

There, in the plane, overwhelmed in the face of it all, I could do no more than utter a small prayer: "Be with them, Lord, all 3.5 million Armenians. Comfort their grief, be merciful to the dead, and remain with the living. Let them perceive Your hand at work in their nation."

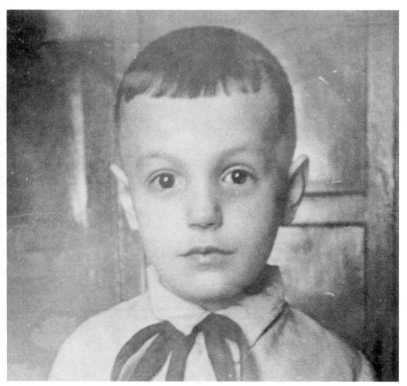

A young Mikhail at age seven (1949).

Hymn-singing at Soviet church. (Photo by Karen Racek.)

St. Basil's Cathedral—Orthodox church in Moscow. (Photo by Karen Racek.)

A closed Orthodox church in Moscow. Note university in the background.
(Photo by Karen Racek.)

Morgulis preaching at Soviet church.

Mikhail with Vasili Logvinenko (and wife)—Pastor of Moscow Baptist Church and President of the All-Union Council of Evangelical Christians–Baptists.

Plaque at Georgian Museum of Culture and Art (a former seminary) commemorating that Joseph Stalin "lived and studied here" for the priesthood from 1894—1899.

Bella Akhmadulina, dubbed "the queen of Russian poetry," relaxes with Mikhail.

From left to right, Grigori Ivanovich Komendant—Ukrainian church leader; Mikhail; Yakov Dukhonchenko—Ukrainian church leader; and Vladimir Yemshinetsky, a popular Soviet actor.

Mikhail recording in Slavic Gospel Association studio in Wheaton, Illinois (April 1989). Recorded weekly, the tapes are broadcast daily on eleven missionary radio stations throughout the world to an estimated audience of 10—12 million people.

Mikhail being introduced at Moscow Baptist Church—August 4, 1988.
(Photo by Karen Racek.)

Mikhail dining with "Mr. What a Country," comedian Yakov Smirnov, in Evanston, Illinois (1988).

Tour group from the Christian Reformed Church's "Back to God Hour," with whom Mikhail made his trip to Soviet Union. Mikhail and his daughter are in the middle of the front row.

CHAPTER EIGHT

A Crimean Chapter: Yalta and Beyond

> Your old friends are your worst
> critics. (From a Russian play)

August 9–11, 1988 . . .

Our next stop was the beautiful land of Crimea. As we flew above its reddish terrain, crisscrossed by rocky ridges and dotted with gardens, I noticed the shores of this lovely land, caressed by the Black Sea.

Crimea is very reminiscent of California. Its ruddy soil is warmed generously by the sun, and it is rich in fruit and vegetables. The warm and gentle Black Sea is the pearl in the crown of Crimea. I know this sea well, for I had come here in my youth and was delighted by its great beauty. I never understood why it earned the name "Black," because usually its color is vibrantly blue, occasionally even emerald.

To Holiday in Yalta

Yalta is the main city and resort in Crimea. A great many prominent Russians have visited Yalta in the past: writers, artists, and musicians. This sun-soaked land seemed to give them a special degree of inspiration; it filled their poetry and music with a unique enchantment. It was also here that "Uncle Joe" Stalin met with Churchill and Roosevelt during World War II to sign the crucial treaty against Hitler.

To holiday in Yalta is the dream of every Soviet citizen. But it is extraordinarily difficult to get here; it is very expensive, and there are simply not enough facilities for would-be vacationers. The best facilities along the shore are taken up by government sanatoriums and houses of rest for the Party elite. There are places for ordinary Soviet tourists here, but the commoners' facilities are way below the standards enjoyed by state functionaries, and there are less of them too.

We were brought to the *Yalta* Hotel. It was built on Stalin's orders in 1936. The main advantage of this hotel is that it faces the beach. The leader of our delegation aptly summed up the *Yalta* Hotel as a "factory of rest."

Looking at it reminded me of another hotel in Yalta which went under the exotic name *Oreanda*. I stayed in the *Oreanda* some seventeen years ago, when I was just a young, struggling writer. It was a time of both joys and sorrows. Later I wrote a story about it called "Death in Yalta," and it was published in one of the leading Russian journals.

I knew, even before we arrived, that the Baptist church in Yalta was having problems completing its building because the authorities were doing everything they could to create difficulties. So the first thing I did was catch a cab and set off to find the pastor. I had no idea that the address I had was an old one. The taxi stopped outside a distinctly lopsided house with sagging walls. I entered in and wandered around a basement communal apartment of a kind I thought no longer existed. The basement was divided up by sheets of plywood into about ten small compartments, each one housing a family. It was damp and smelled of mice. Drunken voices drifted out from behind the partitions. I knocked on one of the partitions and asked for the pastor. There was nothing wrong with the acoustics in the basement, and dozens of voices responded to my query. Actually, all my invisible informants immediately plunged into an argument, each one insisting that his information was correct, and all the others had it wrong. In the end I discovered that nobody really knew the pastor's new address. In great disappointment I had to return to the hotel.

Chance Meetings or Divine Appointments?

As my daughter and I crossed the hotel foyer, speaking English to each other, I was suddenly hailed by an excited cry,

"Misha, Misha! How are you doing?"

It took me a moment to recognize the speaker as an old friend of mine, a well-known Soviet composer. Ten years had passed since we saw each other last. We must have both looked stunned and rather funny.

"You both look as if you've lost something," joked my daughter.

"I suppose it is our youth," I replied.

Other people recognized my friend and started coming up to him for autographs. He is extremely popular in Russia, his songs have been sung by hundreds of Soviet artists, and he has written numerous operas and operettas. I learned that the famous music festival "Crimean Dawns—1988" was taking place in the city. This explained all the hubbub. It had drawn a large number of actors, singers, composers, and musicians. I made arrangements to meet my friend later that evening.

Elated by such an unexpected encounter, I set off across the foyer, only to be hailed again. This time it was a popular comedy actor, another old friend. He was so overwhelmed that he almost wept. As a matter of fact, I wasn't far from tears myself. We had been very close in our youth, knew all each other's secrets, and never thought that fate would part us. We agreed to meet later that evening too.

When I got back to my room, I worked on trying to find the pastor. He had no phone, and I didn't have an exact address. I decided to have a try at finding him through telephone inquiries.

I called the telephone operator without much hope and asked for the number of the Yalta Baptist Church. To my great surprise she had a listing. I dialed immediately and had another stroke of luck—someone picked up the phone. It turned out to be one of the members of the congregation. I didn't go into great detail over the phone, but he caught on very quickly and agreed that I should come over immediately.

The Yalta believers are expanding their ancient church within their own modest means. There is much work to be done as they are virtually building their church anew. All the work is done in the evenings by the members after they have finished their regular daytime jobs. We exchanged embraces with the brethren who had come to the meeting; they told me their news and I answered their questions. It was agreed that our whole group would come to the church the next day.

The Love of God in Another Land

I devoted the evening to meeting my old friends as planned. They pelted me with questions nonstop. They asked about American people, music, culture, and about my own life. We talked and talked, as though there could be no end.

Suddenly one of them, a popular singer, asked, "Tell me truthfully, are you happy in America?"

How does one reply to such a seemingly simple, yet in fact extremely complex question? Can there be a short answer? On this occasion, I said to him, "Unfortunately, there's no such thing as a paradise on earth yet, and probably never will be. There's a drastic shortage of one crucial material for that. America has its drawbacks, but it is a marvelous country. I hold it in deep respect and, I must admit, love it very much."

"I hope, however, you still love Russia."

"Of course I do, and I never forget her. Russia is my first love, and it remains, like every first love, in one's heart forever. But often we love again after our first love, even though we treasure its recollection."

"Tell me," interjected my friend the comedy actor, "I listen to your broadcasts from time to time, and it seems as though you have become a Christian. Is that so? Or do you do Christian broadcasts for the money?"

His question was a typical manifestation of the Soviet mentality. Yet he was asking sincerely, without any desire to take a dig at me. Russians often ask each other questions which would be deemed "tactless" in the West. Take a look at any good Russian book, and you'll see how the characters in it pose such questions to each other. They are trying to get to the root of some truth—"climb into someone's heart, boots and all," as they say. But, I realized, between old friends such questions are natural and acceptable, and they deserve an answer.

"Do you remember," I said, "that I left here because I didn't want to work just for money? I hope you recall that I took nothing with me; I gave away all my possessions. So tell me, what would be the sense in leaving my motherland because I didn't want to just make money and then do precisely that in another country? Of course, everybody needs money, especially in America, but making money isn't my priority. It is about the fourth thing on my list of life's essentials."

"And what are the three you consider more important, then?" the singer asked.

"The love of God, the love of people, and the love of my family."

"Listen to him, will you!" cried my actor friend. "He spoke then like a real believer."

"But you haven't answered my question," interrupted the singer. "Are you happy now or not?"

"You can't be just happy or just unhappy all the time," I countered. "And that's how it is with me too. In recent years I have come to a knowledge of God. I think I have found Him, and He has found me. But that's beside the point: it's just that when I am with Him I'm happy. When I feel love for people, for my neighbors—then I'm happy. I'm happy when I can help someone. In other words, when I love selflessly, I'm happy. But that is not always the case. If I am angry with someone, then I'm miserable. When I forget someone, I'm unhappy, just as when I forget someone who has saved me. And there are times when, like all people, I feel miserable for no obvious reason. Yet, those are the times when I need Him most."

"Need who?" the singer queried.

"Jesus Christ, of course. Who else?"

There was silence in the room. My friends watched me curiously. Finally, the actor spoke, "So you mean to say that you have become a different person?"

"No, of course not. I'm still the same Misha. It's just that something changed in my heart, as though a switch was flipped, and light flooded in. I suppose you could say that I changed in my soul. But I don't really know how to explain it. Only somebody who has experienced the same thing can fully understand such an encounter with God."

"Do you remember anything by memory from the Bible?"

I repeated to them the wise words of Ecclesiastes: "To everything there is a season and a time to every purpose under the heaven; a time to be born and a time to die; a time to plant and a time to pluck up that which is planted; a time to kill and a time to heal; a time to break down and a time to build up; a time to weep and a time to laugh; a time to mourn, and a time to dance; a time to cast away stones and a time to gather stones; a time to embrace, and a time to refrain from embracing; a time to get and a time to lose; a time to keep and a time to cast away; a time to rend and a time to sew; a time to keep silence and a time to speak; a time to love and a time to hate; a time of war and a time of peace" (Ecclesiastes 3:1-8).

Then I read a description of the Crucifixion, and after that, in deepest silence, the beloved 23rd Psalm.

I looked at my friends. They are personalities known to millions of Russian people. Their eyes had lost all wariness, and were full of the old warmth I remember so well. They looked so beautiful in that moment. It seemed to me that the Holy Spirit moved among us in the tense silence.

Sing unto the Lord a New Song

"I'm going to write some music to accompany that psalm," said my composer friend. "At least, I'll try. Gorbachev's right—it's time to stop being afraid. It's not enough to sit around talking and talking, but doing nothing. After all, David himself points the way by saying: 'Whom should I fear . . . ?' "

He then started to sing, and the rest of us joined in. We sang the songs of our youth, about a love which disappears with the coming of the dawn, and another kind of love, which is eternal. The only way to tell which is the one that lasts forever is to find a strange, nameless white flower—which each one of us seeks.

The following day we went to church. There was no bus, so I ordered seven taxis for our group. The driver of my car, a handsome young man, was interested in finding out who we were. I explained.

"Tell your friends," he said unexpectedly, "that I'm a Communist, but I believe in God."

I did so, and my companions, in their turn, were very intrigued. "How can that be?" they wanted to know.

"Personally, I find it easy," said the driver. "Of course, if it were to become known, I might get kicked out of the Party. But I don't go around advertising it. I've only told you because you're Americans. I've served in the army in Afghanistan, but that's a long story, and not one that I feel like going into. What it comes down to, though, is that I was wounded in the stomach by a mine fragment."

He smiled grimly and then went on: "An American-made mine, as it happens."

I retorted that there had been Americans who had been wounded by Soviet-made mines.

"Oh, I'm not complaining: war is war, and everyone uses whatever they've got. Anyway, I was sent back for treatment. I was lucky—the doctors who looked after me were very good. They managed to fix everything, but I still had problems with my liver—they couldn't do anything about that. Then somebody advised me to go and see this old woman, who's a believer. She took one look at me and said: 'I'm going to treat you for a year and a half. In that time, though, you mustn't drink, swear, or commit adultery. And when you're cured, you must thank God.' So I agreed. For the next eighteen months she treated me with all sorts of herbs, and while she did so, she always prayed and always asked Christ for help. And about one and a half years later, I was well again. When she saw this, she said: 'Remember what you have to do now!'

"So I knelt, even though she hadn't asked me to, and said, 'O Lord of heaven and earth, thank You for extending Your grace to me.' And from that time on, I have believed in God."

"Without doubt, God loves you," I said, handing him my Bible. "But if you learn from the Bible why God saves us, you will be able to get help from Him yourself, not only through the intercession of old ladies."

"But it's got your name on it," he said, when he opened it. "I can't take this. It's your personal Bible."

91

"What if it is? Now it will be yours. Maybe it will remind you of my words 'why God saves people.' "

Again, I sensed the Lord working in a marvelous and miraculous way. I left the driver with a prayer on my lips, sure that my God was stronger than any man-made ideology.

Prayer: The Only Foundation

A large group of believers was waiting for us as we arrived at the Yalta church. Despite all the construction, none of the meetings have been disrupted, but continue to take place every Sunday.

We began by praying that the Lord would bless this virtually new house of prayer. We read from the Bible and sang. It's marvelous to hear the same hymn being sung simultaneously in Russian and in English. No interpreters are needed at such times; you simply feel as though your whole soul is singing.

Later we were served cold compote. This is an old Russian favorite, made by stewing dried fruits in lots of liquid. It is specially loved by children.

Moved by their great need, I donated $300 toward the rebuilding of the church, and my American friends immediately raised another $300 among them.

Back in the street, we took another look at the graceful, cream-colored building. A lot of children gathered round; they were followed by adults. We handed out badges and ball-point pens. Suddenly a woman with a tired face brought a three-year-old boy up to us. "Please pray over him," she said. "He's very frail, and his father has deserted us. Pray that he will be comforted, instead of fretting for his father all the time."

We prayed right there in the street. I laid my hand on the child's small, warm head and asked, "Lord, protect him."

In fact, we prayed for all children who have been deserted by their parents, for all small, aching hearts feeling lost and alone in a big world.

Pop Goes the Culture

Before leaving Yalta, my daughter and I managed to make a couple of forays to the crowded beach. The Black Sea embraced us like an old friend. We swam in its azure waters and then stretched out in the sun. On the wooden beach chairs beside us there were two young couples who noticed the English book I had in my hands. Speaking among themselves, they tried to translate the title into Russian, but without much success. I opened one eye and prompted them.

"Are you Russian?" they asked immediately.

"Yes, I am, but I'm from America."

They stared at me as though I were some creature from outer space, a latter-day *ET*. Then, after a moment's silence, came a flood of questions, both comic and serious. Is it true, they wanted to know, that the Ku Klux Klan tries to assassinate Democrats? Is it true that Michael Jackson is about to marry Elizabeth Taylor? Do Reagan and Bush really believe in God? How many cars do I have? Which musical groups are the most popular in the States right now? Is it true that the Russian émigré comedian, Yakov Smirnov, has become a celebrity in America? We answered as best we could, but the last question was of personal concern to me. It caused my mind to wander.

A Friend on Both Sides of the Ocean

The name of the comedian Yakov Smirnov—"What a County!"—is known to many Americans. His jokes are repeated from coast to coast. He frequently appears on TV shows and in commercials.

Yakov and I have known each other about twenty years. In Russia he was a little-known actor, and used to work on cruise ships, entertaining the passengers.

By Soviet theatrical standards, work like this is just about the lowest rung of the ladder of success. At that time, as well as writing stories and articles, I also wrote jokes and monologues for prominent comedy actors because the state concert organizations used to pay for them quite handsomely. Naturally, actors and their agents went to great pains to insure that material written for them would not fall into anyone else's hands. Yakov needed material badly and wrote asking for my help. The state did not want to pay for material for him, and he was in a very tight financial situation. So, in breach of the rules, I began to send him copies of material I had written for others. We reached agreement that if anyone were to catch on to what was happening, he would simply say that he bought the material from some middleman whose name he didn't know.

From that time we became "Misha" and "Yasha" to each other, the diminutives of our full names—Mikhail and Yakov.

Yasha was born in the Black Sea port city of Odessa, a town which has the well-deserved reputation of being the wittiest place in Russia. Like all port cities, Odessa is colorful, noisy, and vital. People in Odessa talk loudly, joke freely, and have a very definitive local accent. The people of Odessa maintain that in their city, everyone jokes: old people, children, women, and men alike. It was out of this environment that Yasha came.

When circumstances brought us both to America, Yakov and I met again in New York a few years ago. Yakov, by that time beginning to work in comedy clubs, said, "Misha, we're in a new country now. Let's work together in this field."

I declined as tactfully as I could. In the end I said, "Yasha, I came here to learn about things of which I knew nothing before. And now I know that life consists of two aspects: the physical and the spiritual. The physical side we all know, but now I want to seek and find the spiritual dimension of our existence. If I succeed, I want to write about it, talk about it, publish books about it. Don't be offended, but I have no desire at all to occupy my time by thinking up jokes."

We both followed our different paths, but we kept in touch, and met from time to time. Soon Yasha was spotted by prominent concert agents and success and big earnings followed swiftly. He has been featured on "Lifestyles of the Rich and Famous." Nowadays Yasha lives in Beverly Hills and drives a Rolls Royce. Despite the change in his fortunes, we still have phoned each other and met, though not as often as before.

Not long ago my wife and I met Yakov and his fiancée for dinner in Chicago. They took us to a noted downtown restaurant. He was recognized, of course, and people kept coming up to ask for his autograph. He acknowledged that he was used to such inconveniences.

"Do you have any regrets about following a different path and going into the Christian ministry field?" Yasha asked me quietly during our meal.

"No," I answered simply.

He sighed. "Oh well, so each of us has found what he was seeking."

Yakov Smirnov, I might mention, has a very reverent attitude toward the Bible. I phoned him once very upset that somebody had stolen three rolls of film I had sent to be developed—films with photos of him, his fiancée, and my children.

At first Yasha joked about it, telling me that laboratory technicians need money too. They didn't steal from malice, he said, but probably to sell the photos to some journal. Then suddenly serious, he said a very interesting thing, "Do you know what the difference between us is? I make people laugh. I distract them from the harsh realities of everyday life. As for you, you want them to think about life. You force them back to face it. And I don't know which one of us is right. Perhaps people need a bit of both."

Standing on the Black Sea beach, I reflected on Yasha's words. His words rang true; people do need a bit of both. But I realized I was almost halfway through my Soviet tour, and I had much yet to accomplish. Yasha could entertain at will now in America, but I had less than two weeks left to fulfill my mission in Russia. With renewed vigor I dedicated myself to going on.

CHAPTER NINE

A Leningrad Legacy

Do you want to hear the truth
about Moscow? Ask the
inhabitants of Leningrad.
(Leningrad resident)

August 12, 1988 . . .

We flew out of Yalta, leaving behind the red, sun-kissed Crimean soil and headed for a wondrous, foggy, and cold city—Leningrad. It was the birthplace of Lenin's Bolshevik revolution, and official Soviet propaganda refers to it as such—"the cradle of the Russian revolution."

To fully appreciate life in Leningrad we must first go on a brief historical detour of this city. One of Russia's most outstanding czars, Peter the First, began his own *perestroika* some 250 years before Gorbachev. He realized that the country would remain backward forever unless sweeping reforms were carried out. Peter's reforms were mainly of an economic nature. He (who came to be known later as "Peter the Great") decided to distance the enormous class of rich and conservative nobility (the boyars) from the seats of power. In the contemporary parlance of Gorbachev's reforms, one might compare this class to the "bureaucratic Party apparatus." In their stead, Peter advanced talented people from the masses; he sent them off to study in Europe. (Unlike the "Soviet czars" of the 20th century, he was not afraid that they would not come back home.) At the same time, he invited an enormous number of foreign military specialists, craftsmen, seamen, and merchants (like today's businessmen—a valuable lesson for Gorbachev!) to come to live and work in Russia. The

97

overwhelming majority of these foreigners came from Germany, and to this day some two million of their descendants still live in the Soviet Union. You will encounter German surnames among Soviet science, agriculture, medicine, and sports.

Peter understood that Russia must develop and broaden contacts with the rest of Europe if economic and cultural progress was to be achieved. At that time, Russia was cut off from her European neighbors not just psychologically, but geographically as well, and needed to find cultural and trade outlets in Europe. The obstacle to this was neighboring Sweden. Peter went to war against the Swedes, emerged victorious, and gained a foothold on the Baltic coast. This marked the beginning of Russia's merging into European civilization. Every Russian schoolchild knows Peter's famous words: "I shall chop a window through into Europe!"

A Window on the West

After his victory over Sweden, Peter decided to build a new city—"a window on the West"—which was given his name—Petersburg. The site chosen for the new city was empty marshland. History recounts that the great reformer built his new city on the bones of hundreds of thousands of serfs who were drafted in to carry out the construction. Peter invited leading European architects and sculptors to take part in the planning of Petersburg, whose symbol became the famous statue of Peter on horseback by the Italian master Falcone.

Petersburg (later Petrograd, then Leningrad) is distinguished by an enormous amount of museums and monuments, but undoubtedly the most famous of these is the Hermitage, whose collections of paintings and other treasures outranks even such famous museums as the Paris Louvre.

There is a very special seasonal phenomenon in Leningrad—the so-called "white nights." This is a time when the streets of Leningrad are bathed by a pale, twilight glow throughout the entire night, and darkness does not fall. The impression this creates is that time has become suspended between day and night. Petersburg and its famous white nights have been lauded in the works of the best Russian poets.

It should be noted that Peter made Petersburg his capital, and so it remained for a long time before Moscow became the "center" again.

As I have already mentioned, Peter joined Russia to Europe and to Western civilization. The cultural and literary heritage of Leningrad continued to exert a great influence on the life and trends of the whole country for a long time. In fact, intellectual inward resistance to Stalin's "Moscow Mafia" lasted longer here than anywhere else. It was not by chance that Stalin and his Leningrad vassal Andrei Zhdanov chose famous Leningrad writers and intellectuals as their first postwar targets for repression—Anna Akhmatova, Mikhail Zoschenko, Mikhail Khazin, and others. A crushing moral blow was delivered to the world-famous composer Dmitri Shostakovich. They were denounced in the press, deprived of a livelihood, and sent to the camps. One of Russia's most brilliant poets to perish in the camps, Osip Mandelstam, addressed his city thus: "Leningrad, I do not want to die yet. I shall return to this city, which is so painfully familiar, like tears, like the smallest vein, like childhood's swollen glands."

A Tale of Two Cities

There is a long-standing rivalry between Moscow and Leningrad—sometimes covert, sometimes overt. It was Leningraders who ironically dubbed Moscow "The Big Village."

The "Northern Palmyra," as Leningrad has been called, was and is the city of the aristocracy, the home of refined Russian culture. The rivalry between the two cities still exists today, albeit on a less exalted plane. For instance, linguists still debate whether "the best and purest" Russian is spoken in Moscow or in Leningrad. May the Muscovites forgive me, but in my opinion Leningrad wins. Not long ago, the widow of the famous writer Vladimir Nabokov (a best-selling author in America in the 1960s) wrote a letter to the press repudiating claims that he was the author of a certain work: "He could not have written this," she asserted, "because he always wrote in impeccable Petersburg Russian."

Many citizens of Leningrad love her to the point of fanaticism. Nobel Prize winner Iosif Brodsky lived in the Vasil-yevsky Island district of Leningrad, and in his early works wrote that this is where he would return to die. Nowadays he lives in New York, but speaking to him on the phone quite recently I thought, these words were not just bravado. I really believe that Iosif would wish to live his last hour in Leningrad. As I watched him receiving the Nobel Prize for literature on television, I was struck by a quirk of history. Several hundred years ago, a Russian czar conquered a Swedish king, yet here was a Swedish king handing a literary award to a Russian poet.

The Times They Are a Changin'

We arrived on a beautiful summer day; the streets and broad avenues of Leningrad were bathed in sunlight. The first port of call was, naturally, the Hermitage. Tourists from all over the world crowded round on all sides, as well as tourists from other Soviet cities. In the hall housing paintings by Leonardo da Vinci I was approached by a local lad aged about fifteen, who offered to exchange a World War II medal for two packs of chewing gum. In my time, something like this would have been punished by a stretch in a juvenile offenders' prison, but *perestroika* must have influenced this sphere of life too. It was not my place to start lecturing him about the respect due to awards won by grandfathers, so all I did, as I gave him some chewing gum, was to ask whether he wasn't afraid of retribu-tion at home.

The youthful entrepreneur seemed genuinely surprised by my query. "Nah," he answered dismissively. "And in any case, if anyone touches me, they'll get as good as they give!"

So here, standing by the immortal works of Leonardo, I caught a glimpse of the contemporary state of the eternal conflict between fathers and sons.

Close by the Hermitage, some enterprising Finnish busi-nessmen had started trading in "American" fast food—hot dogs, hamburgers, and Coca-Cola—but for hard currency only, catering to foreign tourists. Across the road, the locals have to get into a long line to buy *piroshki* (pasties) for rubles. This struck me as offensive, an unconcealed insult to the native population. This may not worry the Finns, but surely the local authorities should be affronted by such undisguised elitism. However, they are not much different. They have everything, be it American or Finnish in origin. To be fair, Gorbachev's reformers are trying to combat this sort of attitude toward the general Soviet public. But Russia is a vast country, the reformers are relatively few in number, and foreign currency is desperately needed.

Walk on the Wild Side

We stayed in the *Pribaltiyskaya* Hotel, which was built by Swedes (another quirk of history!) and one can sense this immediately. A turbulent, clandestine life flourishes around this hotel, just as it does around the *Rossiya* Hotel in Moscow. Money is changed at black-market rates; spirits, cigarettes, and clothing are bought and sold. And, of course, there are prostitutes galore. They are commonly referred to as "hard currency girls," accepting only foreign money in exchange for their services. Their rates go up to $100 a trick, an enormous sum by Soviet standards. At that time, $100 could be changed at a rate of 1 to 9, that is—900 rubles for $100. This is the equivalent of what a Soviet nurse, janitor, or secretary would earn over a period of ten months.

I learned all this and a great deal more from my colleague, a Leningrad journalist who spent a whole day with me. It was he who told me about the unenviable life of Leningrad prostitutes. They have to make regular payoffs to the militia so that they will "turn a blind eye" to their activities, then their pimps pocket the greater part of their earnings in exchange for "protecting" them and finding them customers.

A "hard currency" girl's career ends at the age of twenty-five; after that they are relegated to the ranks of those who are paid in rubles. The situation of the "ruble" prostitutes is much more chaotic than that of their "hard currency" sisters (in fact, this applies to any situation where rubles are the tokens of payment). Increasingly, prostitutes have been victims of violence, and there have been a number of murders.

"There are any number of such cases," said my journalist

friend, "but it is only in recent months that we have been able to write a little about them, and very cautiously at that. For many Soviet citizens it was an eye-opener—they had been convinced that this problem didn't exist here, but in fact it has, and for a very long time. The truth of the matter is that prostitution was never eradicated. And don't we have people suffering from AIDS too? But that's 'thanks' to foreign tourists."

However, I protested at this point, arguing that the AIDS virus could have reached the Soviet Union just as easily through Soviet citizens returning from abroad.

The Spirit Moves

After this discussion, I felt a special need to go to church. The Protestant church in Leningrad is located on the ancient *Poklonnaya* Hill, a place where people gathered to pray over the centuries. That is how this hill got its name—it derives from the Russian verb "to bow down."

The church was packed. I was invited to take the service, and allotted the traditional "Russian hour"—that is, talk for as long as you like. The choir wore special robes and sang with inspiration and beauty.

I was surrounded by hundreds of people, whose shining faces showed clearly how they were uplifted by the singing. I noticed a man of about thirty who stood on the balcony; he had a long beard, and his enormous eyes seemed to burn with particular fervor. He reminded me of the great Russian Christian writer, Fyodor Dostoyevsky.

I spoke again of the sufferings of Christ, our own sufferings, and about life in Christ. As I preached, in my mind's eye I had a clear picture of the passion of our Lord as it is described in the Bible. I saw before me, quite clearly, a dark cross with the body of the Saviour crucified on it.

A buzzing of voices filled the church by the end of the address; there were sounds of weeping. Suddenly, a man and woman forced their way forward and fell to their knees. The man cried out, almost shouting, "Lord, Thou hast rent the shroud of darkness!" Tears poured down the woman's face.

Later, someone told me about this couple. He is a university professor who lectures on the history of culture, and his wife is a teacher of French. They had been passing by the church, but when they saw so many people gathered together, decided to find out what was going on. They were told that a believer from America would be preaching, and they decided to stay for a few minutes and listen to what this foreigner had to say. But the Lord had a different plan, and an hour later they were on their knees before Him. Again, I was overwhelmed with the way that God's Spirit had worked. A chance meeting attended led to a life-changing commitment.

After the service I was once again grasped by hundreds of friendly hands, extending greetings and pushing notes into my pocket. Later, I found money in my pockets as well and wondered what on earth I should do with it. Finally, I decided to distribute it among those believers who were in need.

I noticed an elderly woman who remained seated away from everyone else, all alone, staring straight ahead. I made my way over to her, and she lifted her eyes and spoke.

"Brother Mikhail, I prayed that you would come up to me. I have been praying for your mission [SGA] for fourteen years now. Last night I asked God to give you some special words to say to us."

And it occurred to me that maybe that was why I had found it so easy to speak today. Then I noticed that she could not move her feet.

"I have been paralyzed for many years," she said, seeing the direction of my glance. "Friends brought me here. Please pass on my warmest greetings to your Joni Eareckson Tada. I always pray for her too."

Several months later I was able to fulfill this request.

Encounter at Granny's Garden
That evening I went to a Leningrad park which is popularly known as "Granny's Garden." In these times of *glasnost* it has become a venue for public discussions, and Leningrad citizens, hungering after freedom of expression, meet here in a kind of Soviet version of the famous Speakers' Corner in London's Hyde Park. Some 400 people had gathered there that evening.

A morose, curly-haired young man strummed a guitar and sang lugubriously that "this land has been forgotten by both God and the devil."

I raised an objection. "If you mean Russia," I said, "then I don't agree with you. God has never forgotten Russia."

"No, I mean Afghanistan. I fought there."

Four militiamen stood a little removed from the milling throng of people, making no attempt to interfere. When I lived here some ten years ago, this would have seemed unimaginable.

"Tell me," I asked them, "how do you find your job these days? Before, all you had to do was follow orders, but now you probably have to make independent decisions."

To my surprise, they responded. Admittedly, one of them did most of the talking, the one who seemed to be the best "briefed."

Our conversation attracted attention, and more and more people began drifting over to listen. Most of them eyed the American flag badge pinned to my coat, and I heard a young boy call excitedly to his friend, "Vitya, come here, quick, an American's going to say something!"

In an amazingly short period of time, I found myself surrounded by 400 people who were burning with curiosity to hear what this American would have to say. I was even asked to climb up on the pedestal of a rather battered statue of some Greek goddess. Side by side with this unknown deity, I could not help but remember Paul's preaching at Mars Hill in the Book of Acts. I began to answer questions. They came in a flood lasting two hours.

Toward the end I was interrupted by the young man who had fought in Afghanistan. "Hey, fellow, why don't you tell us instead about our soldiers who went from captivity to live in America? How are they making out?" (The question referred to Russian prisoners of war in Afghanistan who were released to Amnesty International in the United States.)

I replied that I could speak about only two of them. One, Nikolai Ryzhkov, decided finally to go back to the Soviet Union, and was sentenced to twelve years in hard labor camps, even though the Soviet ambassador in Washington had assured him that nothing would happen to him. However, not long ago *perestroika* affected his fate too, and he was released. The other one, Nikolai's friend, decided against returning, abandoned a way of life that consisted largely of public appearances in front of Americans and sampling every sort of vodka imaginable, and enrolled in college. As far as I know, he lives somewhere in Pennsylvania.

Freedom for the Captives

The former Soviet ambassador in Washington, Oleg Troyanovsky, gave Nikolai Ryzhkov his personal guarantee that nothing would happen to him if he went back to Russia.

However, as we know, Ryzhkov was promptly put on trial when he returned to the Soviet Union, and sentenced to twelve years in the camps. He served three years of this sentence before being released in the unofficial Gorbachev amnesty. Strangely enough, a law has been enacted since that time, according to which desertion from the Soviet army in Afghanistan no longer qualifies as "treason against the motherland."

In passing, it should be noted that the draconian law which equated captivity with treason existed in the Soviet Union since the World War II and was the brainchild of that "great humanitarian," Joseph Stalin. As a result of this, the camps of the "Gulag Archipelago" were swelled by millions of Soviet soldiers who had been captured by the Germans, and for this "crime" were transported from German concentration camps into Soviet ones.

Personally, I think that Troyanovsky may have really believed that Ryzhkov would not be punished. But there was no hint of *glasnost* at that time, and the KGB could not have cared less about what some Soviet ambassador had said abroad.

I related a little of this information in the Leningrad "Granny's Garden," and nobody tried to silence me, accuse me of being a spy, or drag me off to the nearest militia precinct. In other words, nobody made any move to do the expected, what the Soviet regime would call for (and always did). This gives me hope that the changes taking place in Russia now are not just a modernization of the system, but its gradual deposition. Admittedly, at the same time in other cities, the local authorities are doing their utmost to crush any popular manifestations of freedom. For instance, public meetings were broken up brutally not so long ago in Minsk (Byelorussia), Riga (Latvia), and Erevan (Armenia).

A Startling Speech Is Secured

While addressing the throngs, an overwhelming feeling of anxiety came over me. There were a few moments during which it seemed like the crowd gathered around me had merged into a single body. Awakened from earlier fears, the faces around me looked decisive and prepared for action. The body of the crowd seemed to sway and eddy; dozens of eyes watched me with curiosity but, at the same time, grimly and threateningly. Of course, any reforms free people from bondage and give them the opportunity to transform themselves into something else. But very often, calls for freedom give birth to death and destruction. The example of the French revolution comes easily to mind, and also what happened here, in Russia, a mere seventy years ago. May God forgive me, but in those moments I felt that if just one strong and commanding person had urged that crowd to loot, burn, and kill, it would probably have done so without a qualm.

After answering hundreds of questions, I was hoarse and exhausted. I started trying to force my way out of the crowd. People continued to pelt me with questions as I passed and they pressed bits of paper into my hands. Two young men about thirty years of age managed to separate me from the surrounding press of humanity. They said quietly, "We belong to the 'separate' church. There's a document we'd like to show you. Will you come with us?"

"No," I said, prompted by some instinct of caution, "let's go to my hotel."

My suspicions, however, proved groundless. They really were what they claimed to be. Churches in the Soviet Union are divided into registered (that is, officially approved) and unregistered (sometimes called "catacomb") congregations. Some years ago, a number of these unregistered churches began to function openly, but refused to merge with their registered fellow believers. So they became autonomous—that is, independent of both the registered and the unregistered congregations.

It would not have been advisable for them to go to a hotel catering to the foreign tourist trade because there are always plainclothes KGB men on duty in the foyers of such hotels, and the doormen are all voluntary informers. So we decided to go to the railway station and talk there.

We found a quiet but dingy spot in the general waiting hall. In an atmosphere that reeked of human sweat and cheap cigarettes, they handed me a sheaf of closely typed sheets.

"This is a secret speech delivered by the Chairman of the Council for Religious Affairs, Konstantin Kharchev, to graduates of the Higher Party School in Moscow," they told me.

This school plays a very significant role in Party policy. The institution teaches Communists who occupy high Party posts, and who, after graduation, go on to even more senior Party positions.

The document shown to me was of particular interest because it contained a record of Kharchev talking uninhibitedly to his Party comrades, not to foreigners or religious believers. I have already noted that I found Kharchev's public demeanor pleasant, but the text of his speech proved the truth known to many of the faithful: the Soviet authorities only tolerate Christ and His followers to the degree they deem expedient and are unremitting in their efforts to control them.

The undoubtedly intelligent and forthcoming Kharchev knows much, but I believe that there is one thing that he has not been able to understand: that someone who has sincerely accepted Christ, and who has dedicated his life to Him, can only submit to Christ's control and none other.

I think that this "secret" speech of Kharchev's delivered at the end of March 1988 is a unique document; therefore I have reproduced it with only very minor revisions.[1] I am grateful to my comrade, Nikodino, who took great risk to deliver the speech to me and so give opportunity for it to be published in the West.

I was informed by a reliable source that when Kharchev learned that a transcript of his speech had reached the West, he exclaimed in frustration, "What are things coming to? It's not even safe to speak openly in the Party School!"

[1]The text of Kharchev's speech can be found in the Appendix.

CHAPTER TEN

More Lessons in Leningrad

Live a century, learn a century.
(Russian saying)

August 13, 1988 . . .

The next day I went to Leningrad Baptist toward the end of a church meeting, as I had an appointment to meet their young people. Since my meeting was informal, I wore jeans and sneakers. I found a place at the back, and turned my attention to listening to the elderly preacher who was addressing the congregation. All of a sudden, there was unexpected movement around the front pulpit. Someone recognized me, and several people came down to lead me to the front of the church. I must confess I had some misgivings. The way I was dressed was highly unsuitable for speaking in a Russian church!

The local believers are extremely strict about such matters. In many churches the women are seated separately and must always have their heads covered. Jewelry and cosmetics are frowned on, and even those who are "guilty" of wearing wedding rings have to put up with fire and brimstone being rained down on them from the pulpit. I remarked to one young believer that, in my opinion, it is not the sight of a wedding ring that leads to temptation, but the absence of one. A married woman with nothing to identify her status must expect to be approached by men seeking to make her acquaintance. He agreed with me, and said that his wife frequently found herself in such a situation. But, he added with a deep sigh, he just couldn't muster up the courage to go against what has become an accepted tradition. In provincial churches it is not unknown for the older women to take a ruler and, in front of the whole congregation, measure the length of some girl's blouse and then declare: "Sister, this is indecent in the eyes of the Lord! Next time, make sure you wear something with longer sleeves!"

The men traditionally dress in black suits and white shirts, and in most cases, with no tie. That was why I felt so uneasy standing up at the front of the church dressed in jeans, a T-shirt, and sneakers. (Thank heaven, the T-shirt at least was black!)

The elderly preacher concluded what he was saying very quickly, and the pastor called my name. I went up to the pulpit and asked, "What do you want me to do?"

"Carry on the service," he replied calmly, and added the customary query, "Will an hour be enough?"

I began by apologizing to the congregation for my overly casual garb. They seemed to take it in stride. Then I addressed myself to the Lord praying, "Show me, O Lord, the right place in Thy Word for these people!"

Lord, Let Your Servant Speak

As I started to speak, down below and to my left I saw three young men who were greatly pleased that I had unwittingly flouted local church conventions and was preaching while wearing jeans. As I looked at them, a chord of memory stirred in my mind, and I remembered the story from the Book of Daniel about the three youths Shadrach, Meshach, and Abednego.

I then refocused my thoughts and addressed the crowd. As I looked at the several thousand faces turned toward me I explained that my topic would be the testing of faith. I told them the story of Nebuchadnezzar in which they could all easily recognize the persecutors of Russian Christians—those who serve only Caesar in the words and actions of informers, passing themselves off as Christians. We are frequently urged to pay homage to the golden idol, and it is very easy to avoid punishment merely by bending the knee. Dolores Ibarrui, who through the wiles of fate became a revolutionary, once said that it is "better to die on your feet than to live on your knees." And this maxim is one that applies very well to the life of believers.

I asked them to remember what Nebuchadnezzar saw when he looked into the furnace—that there was someone else in there with the miraculously unharmed three Hebrew boys: someone described in the Bible as like "the Son of man."

I proclaimed, "I am willing to observe the laws of the land in which I live, even though I may not like some of them. But there is one law to which I will never submit: that is a law which would require me to pay homage to an idol instead of standing face-to-face with the Living God. The fiery furnace is a test for our faith—yet Christ stands beside us during this trial."

These are the lines along which I addressed that Leningrad congregation. I then turned to prayer for the sake of the children, who must make the difficult choice whether to pay homage to God or to idols. By the tears and forceful prayers of the congregation, I realized that this is a vital issue not just in America, but in Russia too. As Jesus said, "Suffer little children, and forbid them not, to come unto Me: for of such is the kingdom of heaven" (Matthew 19:14).

Christian Literature in Russia

Afterward, I had a meeting with the young people, some sixty or seventy of them. I was particularly impressed by their ability to combine romanticism with action. They do not only talk and dream—they get down to business. For instance, they have acquired the necessary audio equipment to record and reproduce Christian cassettes; they have formed several musical groups and record and disseminate their songs. Our discussion centered around complex spiritual issues, but we also touched on literature and art. We had a very stimulating discussion about the books issued by our Slavic Gospel Press (SGP) publications. It was very heartening for me to see how many of these young, intelligent Russian Christians had read our translated editions of C.S. Lewis, G.K. Chesterton, Francis Schaeffer, Josh McDowell, Billy Graham, F.F. Bruce, and other outstanding authors.

I remember how much effort it cost us to insure our publication of the leading Christian writers and to monitor the quality of the translations. There were many initial difficulties, but the reward was that our publications reached a truly professional level. The young believers in Leningrad repeated an observation I had heard in other Russian cities. They felt that a great deal of the Russian language religious literature published in the West is frequently oversimplistic and weak in content. The spiritual level of some of these works is a downright insult to one's intelligence.

I could only agree with them, but added, "Dear friends, I am only the senior editor of SGP, not of all the missions engaged in producing literature in Russian. In America, we have freedom of action, and in the literary field this can often mean temptation to publish questionable items. For instance, you may burn with the desire to enlighten the world with something or other you have written yourself—and if you have the necessary finances at your disposal, then you can insure that your book will be published, never mind who is the greatest beneficiary—the world or the author! There is no centralized administration of publications in America as there is in the USSR, so one publisher cannot dictate to another what to print."

However, I had to admit to the young people that I am pained by every poorly written Christian book. I don't think I am greedy by nature, but I honestly begrudge every penny spent on rubbish which is not worth the paper on which it is printed. This sort of stuff, sent into the land which produced Tolstoy and Dostoyevsky, causes satanic laughter in the ranks of the atheists. Satan rubs his hands with glee, and understandably so, for there is nothing more destructive than tackling serious subjects on a level that renders them absurd. Alas, this is the case with far too many Russian-language books published in America. Unfortunately, they are produced by persons of limited education, with no literary experience, and with a woefully inadequate knowledge of Russian. I never cease to be amazed by the reasoning of some American Christian leaders, who assume that just because someone speaks Russian, that they are equal to the task in question. I am always moved to ask them whether they consider that everyone who speaks English is automatically capable of producing books in that language.

I have even found Bibles that are printed with errors! Does not Christ warrant a greater degree of respect than that? I maintain that everything concerning Him deserves only the best and greatest efforts. Possibly the trouble is that persons who take up a job for which they are eminently unsuitable have little fear of God. It never enters their heads that every distorted Christian book is a sin before God. The fruits of this sin are reaped by Russian believers and nonbelievers who are seeking for spiritual meaning in this difficult life on earth.

"Please don't misunderstand us," said a young university student, "but we find it impossible to offer nonbelievers a great many of the Christian books published in the West. Their low level of quality only turns people off. When you go back to America, please explain to other publishers who we are and what we're like."

I promised them I would carry their message to the West. And I do try, to the best of my ability, but someone devoid of fear of God is not likely to pay much attention. I find myself caught up in a kind of vicious circle. Such writers and publishers are far removed psychologically from life in Russia; they have no feel for the subtleties of the language, and despite their abysmally low intellectual level, they are extremely cocksure and self-satisfied. They neither know nor care that they are dealing a body blow to religious literature, to spiritual thought, and to the Russian language. And if they do not understand this, how can they feel fear of God? The students recognized the problem and understood my frustrations.

The Power of the Printed Word

As we continued our discussion, we devoted quite a lot of time to talking about the work of C.S. Lewis. Lewis' rugged, intellectual apologetics have great appeal to the thoughtful Russian audience. I read a fifteen-minute overview of those of his books which we (SGP) have published in Russian translation: *The Screwtape Letters; Mere Christianity; The Problem of Pain;* and four children's books—*The Lion, the Witch and the Wardrobe; The Silver Chair; The Magician's Nephew;* and *Prince Caspian.* I told them about Lewis' life, his concept of Christianity, and his brief, bittersweet marriage, late in life, to a woman who died of cancer. I also described our future publication plans at SGP.

One of our translations, *Evidence that Demands a Verdict,* has become an unofficial best-seller in Russia. It took two translators a year to complete the Russian edition. I learned that this work is used as a textbook in the Russian Orthodox Seminary in Zagorsk, near Moscow. It is also used as an aid to independent Bible study by Catholic, Russian Orthodox, and Protestant study groups which have sprung up like mushrooms in the rainy climate of *glasnost* and *perestroika.*

I was very interested to learn too that a group of young believers in the town of Zbruisk formed a Christian club called "Pain" after reading Lewis' *The Problem of Pain.* At their meetings they study descriptions of pain in the Bible, the pain suffered by Christ, and the general significance of pain as an integral part of the Christian endeavor.

These literary discussions reinforced my conviction that the fate of a book is an uncontrollable phenomenon. A book is like atomic energy: it can heal or destroy. Those of us who are involved in publication must be ever mindful of our duty to God and people. This is especially true of Russia where a book is very often the only authoritative source of instruction.

In talking with the young people in Leningrad, I was pleasantly surprised to see a significant change in the ten years since I left Russia. Their interests, knowledge of literature, culture, and the humanities is immeasurably superior to those of their contemporaries abroad. In recent years, the authorities have stopped barring young believers from higher education. In earlier times, they had no hope of being admitted into tertiary institutions.

The main stimulus behind their spiritual and intellectual growth has been an insatiable thirst for self-education. It should be noted that this is a traditional characteristic and a most effective method of achievement among the believing Russian intelligentsia. Libraries are full of believers seeking out sources on biblical history, the history of Christianity, and world history. For this reason alone it is not fitting for publishers to deceive them with spiritual skim milk.

Challenged and convicted by my meeting with the youth, I could not help recalling how I was once visited in New York by Peter Deyneka, Jr. and Andrew Semenchuk of Slavic Gospel Association.

"Misha," they said to me, "you frequently conduct worship services before hundreds of people. We're offering you the chance to serve God before millions. We would like you to take on responsibility for the production of quality Christian books and to do radio broadcasts."

I responded to their offer and God's call, gave up a good-paying job and settled way of life, and moved to the town of Wheaton, Illinois, where SGP has operated for the past 15 years.

I had already known that our books were read and valued in Russia, but it was only here, in talking with hundreds of people, that I realized the full extent of their influence on human lives. From letters received daily from listeners I had known that my radio broadcasts had an extensive audience, but it was highly gratifying to find out in person how popular these broadcasts are.

I remember well the Irpen Baptist Church pastor who remarked, "You will never know how many people have stepped on to the path of spiritual freedom in Christ because of those broadcasts."

His testimony was another sign to me of God's hand at work in the land of my first love.

CHAPTER ELEVEN

Kiev: Return to My Home

On home turf, a sparrow is a little
nightingale. (Russian saying)

August 14–18, 1988 . . .

There are some things about which it is both easy and difficult
to write. They are easy because you know them so well—
every ripple of memory, every sound from the past is painfully
familiar and triggers off a world of recollections. Yet for this
very reason, it is hard to write about them too, for you become full to overflowing. Memory resurrects so many vivid
pictures that it is hard to know where to begin and what to
say, for you want to tell everything. Such is how I feel about
my former hometown of Kiev.

The Father of Russian Cities

Kiev is the most ancient city of contemporary Russia. It was
founded 1,500 years ago. Moscow, by comparison, was founded only 800 years ago. Kiev is known as "the father of Russian
cities." It was here that the tribes of Rus became Christians.
Led by Vladimir, the Grand Duke of Kiev, the people living
here abandoned paganism for Christianity 1,000 years ago.
The people of Kiev were baptized in the waters of the beautiful Dnieper River. In memory of this event, an impressive
statue of Vladimir holding aloft a cross towers over the city
from the top of one of the surrounding hills above the river.
This monument can be seen from passing trains, ships, and
planes. The hill is famed throughout Russia. In honor of the

Grand Duke, who was glorified as a saint by the Russian Orthodox Church, it is called Vladimir's Hill.

Over the seventy years of the current Soviet regime, a great many Christian monuments have been destroyed. That makes the survival of this monument to Christianity even more inexplicable. Stalin, Khruschev, and other 20th-century pharaohs ruthlessly blew up and eradicated churches and monuments of much lesser significance. Yet Vladimir remained, towering untouched above the howls and fury of atheist blasphemy, blessing the people with the holy cross. Many people explain this simply: God willed it so. I agree with them. My friend, the outstanding Russian poetess Irina Ratushinskaya, who served more than four years of a twelve-year sentence in Soviet hard-labor camps for writing allegedly "slanderous" poetry, ends the poem she dedicated to the Christianization of Russia with the words: "Do not tire, baptizer Vladimir, Of holding your cross between us and the skies!"

Kiev stands out among the many unique towns of Russia by its unique, gentle enchantment. It is a natural wonder. It consists of hills, parks, woodlands, churches, and streets which climb steeply, and then plunge down toward the river. The city abounds with greenery and flowers. All this green and white beauty is surrounded by the blue girdle of the ancient Dnieper. The ninety-seven-meter-high belfry of the Kiev Monastery of the Caves rears high above the river. This monastery is one of the oldest in Europe. Cities are like people, and in its 1,500-year lifetime Kiev has known both joys and sorrows. It was attacked by enemies on numerous occasions; it was razed and burned. Yet each time it rose again and, strangely enough—every time it grew more beautiful than before.

Legend has it that Kiev was founded by three brothers: Kiy, Khorev, and Schyok, taking its name from the eldest, Kiy. It was here that the beginnings of the future great Russian culture were forged.

Return to My Youth

Years ago as a Kiev resident I lived on the famous Pochaina Street, so named after the river which used to run here.

The Pochaina River was named after the sister of Kiev's three founders. According to ancient legends, Pochaina was a stunningly beautiful, but extremely proud girl. She was besieged by suitors, but thought that none of them were good enough for her. Then as the years slipped by, her would-be suitors no longer beat a path to her door. Realizing her folly, Pochaina was overcome by grief. She climbed a hill, and sat there, weeping bitterly. Legend says she wept so much that her tears formed a river. The street on which I lived so many centuries later is said to follow the course of that one-time river of tears shed by the proud and foolish Pochaina.

One of the oldest surviving churches of Kiev stood—and, thank God, still stands—on our street, the 15th-century church of St. Elijah the Prophet. I recall as a child climbing over the surrounding fence, and running around the church's overgrown yard. One day we were approached by a little, old, sad-eyed priest. In those days the church was boarded up, and no services were permitted in it. (Much later I learned that at that time, the fate of the church hung in the balance—the authorities were deciding whether it should be demolished, or allowed to stand silent without a congregation.) What did the priest think, looking at us, who were taught at school that there is no God, and that all priests are deceivers? His dry old lips moved slightly as he whispered over and over: "Be ye like children. . . . Be ye like children. . . ." We thought that he must be crazy and jeered at him.

It was only many years later that I found out that the words he kept repeating were those of Christ. That wise old man saw that Stalin's regime was turning children into unthinking beasts. He was praying that we would remain children and not become animals.

As a grown man, though I had not yet come to faith, I often made my way to this church on the banks of the Dnieper. There was a strange attraction about the church and I frequented her property in times of defeat and depression.

Now here I was again in this city of museums, flowers, churches, gardens, the city of my childhood and youth, joys and sorrows.

Once I was asked to give a definition of Kiev in one sentence. My answer was that it is a place where it is marvelous to live and terrible to work. In preceding decades Kiev had one of the most stubborn and ossified bureaucracies in all of the Soviet Union, and its courts pronounced draconian sentences on believers and unbelievers alike. There was less freedom and more KGB here than elsewhere. Even nowadays, KGB officials boast openly: "There's no *glasnost* here; we still have firm Soviet government!"

Yet despite the pains and disappointments of the past—Kiev is my city, and I love it. I often dream that I am back here. Kiev figures prominently in my memories of Russia and the short stories I write.

Currents of Memories

As we began our tour of the city, I showed my daughter the streets and houses where part of my life had passed. It was a strange but wonderful sojourn. It seemed as if the city still bore an invisible imprint of my breath, my hopes, my griefs, and my not very cheerful smiles. A great deal of this was beyond her understanding, for who can see entirely into another's soul, be they ever so close? I showed her the hospital where she was born while I spent the night outside waiting. I took her to places where her mother and I used to meet. We strolled down the *Kreschatik,* the central street of Kiev, with its rows of chestnut trees. Bright poppies were splashes of color on all sides, and fountains tinkled gently around us.

I thought, Lord, ten long years have passed since I said good-bye to all this! Yet how quickly those years have flown. The ancients were right when they counseled us to fear time, even if it smiles on us. Everything seemed to be just as it was, but for the fact that a sixteen-year-old daughter now walked by my side, and I was now an American citizen of Russian origin—a visitor, no longer a resident.

Meeting the Ukrainian Baptists

In Kiev airport we were met by Grigori Ivanovich Komendant, the deputy presbyter of the Ukrainian Baptists, and his wife.

As always, he was the soul of kindness. As always, he looked exhausted. Grigori Komendant is a little over forty, and he belongs to what is called the "new generation" of churchmen. He manages to combine gifted preaching and an exceptional knowledge of the Bible with a businesslike, organized approach which results in highly effective service. The bouquet of roses with which he greeted us were the first flowers we received in my hometown. On subsequent days, our hotel rooms were filled to overflowing with flowers given by believers, by old and new friends, and quite often—by total strangers.

On the following day we were received in the Ukrainian Council of Churches. This Council is headed by Yakov Dukhonchenko, the senior presbyter in the Ukraine, whom I had met on many occasions at various international conferences.

Dukhonchenko is a large, heavy man, with lively, penetrating eyes, an unfailing sense of humor, and an ability to be himself in any situation. He spent five years in the camps under Stalin, and after that, devoted his whole life to the activities of the registered churches. I believe that Yakov Dukhonchenko has surely done a great deal for the benefit of both the state and the Ukrainian evangelical brethren.

Fifty percent of all the evangelical churches in the Soviet Union are to be found on the territory of the Ukrainian republic. Pastor Dukhonchenko was instrumental in the opening of many of these churches, and in the import of religious literature into the USSR. At the risk of offending the churches in other towns, I would say that evangelical Christianity is more vital in Kiev, in Ukraine, than anywhere else in the Soviet Union. As I have already mentioned, there is only one Protestant church in Moscow, with its population of 8 million. Kiev's population is a mere 2.5 million, yet it boasts six evangelical churches. The activity here is incessant. A new building is in the process of construction in the *Svyatoshinsky* district, and I went to have a look at it. How pleasant it was to run my hand down the concrete piles of a new church!

I also met with representatives of the unregistered Ukrainian Baptists. They asked me sternly how it came about that I

121

was associating with the leadership of the registered congregations. I replied that I wanted to meet everyone, talk to everyone, witness to everyone, and share my thoughts on spiritual matters with anyone who would listen.

In the life to come, God is not going to divide us up into registered or unregistered Christians, into Baptists, Orthodox, Reformed, or Pentecostals. He will divide us only into those who carried Him in their hearts, and those who did not. This was the conviction I tried to apply in my dealings with all people on my trip.

Ministry in Kiev

In Kiev I served in two churches, even though I was invited to appear in all six. However, there simply was not enough time. One of the churches was the Baptist church on Yamskaya Street.

As I stood in the pulpit of the church, I was surrounded by kind faces and smiling, gentle eyes. They did not address me formally as Mikhail here—to them I was "Misha," a local lad, and this seemed to please them inordinately. This meeting was attended not just by the local congregation, but by nonbelievers and unregistered faithful as well. My address centered, once more, on the issues of pain and love. I recalled an ancient legend I had heard once in an obscure Russian village, and then, many years later, in France.

This legend is about a widow, who had an only son. He grew up handsome and brave, and his mother loved him dearly. Then the son fell in love with a cruel and jealous maiden. Her possessiveness was like a snake, coiling in her heart. She could not bear the thought that her beloved should care for anyone but her, even for his mother. So she said to him: "Dearest, prove how much you love me: if you really love me as much as you say, bring me your mother's heart!" The infatuated young man ran home, plunged a knife into his mother's breast, tore out her heart, and whirled round to take it to his beloved. But as he reached the threshold he tripped and fell. Then he heard his dying mother's voice, "My son, my dear child, you have hurt yourself. I'm so sorry."

I heard the sound of stifled weeping in the church, and continued:

But even such selfless maternal love cannot be compared to the love that Christ has for us. We hear this tale, and we are moved to tears. We can picture it clearly; we have a human understanding of it. It is our misfortune that we people can never fully comprehend the true depth of the sufferings of Christ. And herein lies our temptation—for without fully appreciating this depth, it is hard for us to believe that such a pain could have been. Was it not the Israelites of old who said that the greatest pain is the one that cannot be fully conveyed? Even those closest to us cannot share our pain in its entirety, be they our wife, our husband, our children, or our parents. Only God can share the fullness of our pain. This was accomplished in Christ who was nailed to the cross by human hands.

I called on the Holy Spirit to be with us in our midst. Far up the aisle I could see a man who was clearly torn by conflicting desires and doubts. Several times, he took a couple of steps forward, as though to come up to the pulpit, but then drew back. I came down from the platform, walked up to him, took him by the hand and brought him forward. We both knelt. If you could have only heard how he asked God's forgiveness for his sin. I shall never forget how he moaned and wept.

I must admit that I find it very difficult to come to terms with tears, especially when it is a man crying. Some inward instinct makes me feel that this expresses a loss of male dignity. But at that very moment I realized that we could never lose our dignity in the eyes of God. I did not know what to say to him. I just put my arm around him and joined my prayers to his.

Later about a dozen others came forward, knelt, and prayed. I particularly recall an elderly man with strong, workman's hands praying, "Lord, forgive me for having hated my sister for so long! I loathed her greed and meanness, but now that I am with You, I love her."

It was another stirring service and God's special presence

was evident again, but for some reason I found myself thinking: Lord, I am not worthy of Your grace. Just see how they are all listening to me. I think I understand. You have brought me into the house of the pharaoh to talk about You.

Climbing the Ladder of Love

As usual, in leaving the service, it took us a long time to get back to our car. Many women asked me to pray for their children. I tried to look into the eyes of each one and faithfully pray. Suddenly, a small, squat woman, with dark hair and burning eyes barred my path.

"Keep going, don't stop; she's ill," whispered someone behind me.

However, I stopped. As I did I noticed a rank odor which emanated from the woman's body. Her lips opened to show a mouthful of rotten teeth. Her yellowish, parchment-like skin was covered with festering pustules.

"Do you love me?" she demanded challengingly.

"Christ loves you," I answered.

"But if you don't love me, that means you don't love Christ!" she retorted.

"Christ loves you," I repeated.

"If you love Christ, then you must love me too. If you love Christ, kiss me."

In a blinding flash, it was brought home to me just how hard it is to practice what we preach, to do in reality what we understand in theory. How many of us theoretical Christians there are! Slowly I turned and kissed her.

"Do you love me?" she asked again.

"Please pray for me," I simply answered. "Ask God to give me more love."

I believe that the Christian life means a continuous climb up the ladder of love, at the top of which stands Jesus Christ. When we place our foot on the bottom rung of this ladder, it is very easy for us to love. Because on that lowest rung we love those who are closest to us. The second rung is easy too—for on it we love our friends, who love us in return. The third rung is much harder, but not impossible. At this point we must love our physical neighbors, people with whom we are not closely acquainted and about whom we know little. The next rung is really very difficult, for it entails loving our enemies. Even so, that is still only a beginning, because the higher you rise, the more hateful are the enemies whom you must love. Our hearts protest, and are filled with rejection from a human point of view. Yet we raise our eyes, and see just how much higher we have to climb to reach our Lord.

We shall never reach the top rung, but the very essence of Christ is such that we must continually keep climbing higher and higher up this ladder of love. This is the teaching of Christ and the duty of each of His followers.

Late that evening I met with some friends in an apartment kitchen—a traditional Soviet forum for discussion. One of them, a well-known journalist, had accompanied me anonymously that day to church. He told me that he had deserted his wife and son several years ago. The reason was a common one—he had fallen madly in love with another woman. Typically, this fiery love burnt out quickly, like a bundle of dry kindling. However, he found it impossible to return to his wife and was now all alone.

"Of course, I know that I caused a lot of pain to many people," he said. "Nevertheless, I don't regret anything because the short affair was the happiest time of my life." It occurred to me that he would not have acted that way had he been a believer.

There was so much to discuss, so many memories to relive! As is usual on such occasions, the talk ranged back and forth, noisily and disjointedly. It is strange how we tried to recall only that which was funny and how things that had seemed funny once, now seemed sad.

One young woman, who had been a friend years ago, leaned across the table and asked quietly, "Misha, do you regret leaving?"

It was not easy to give a definitive answer to such a direct question, especially in the hush which suddenly descended around the table. A host of well-known eyes were turned on me, waiting for my reply.

Finally I responded: "If life here was to consist only of such days as today," I said, "of course, I would regret it. But I have wonderful days in America too, days filled with marvelous events, so I do not even think of regrets. Moreover, I frequently say to God: 'Thank You, Lord, for bringing me out.' "

"But don't you want to come back, now that things here are improving?" she inquired.

"From time to time, yes, of course. More so now, than before. I would like to come back, but not forever. And I may be back again; I don't know. I'll come again if the thaw is not halted, if I can do here what I do in America. But to tell you the truth, I'm afraid I would soon start to miss the adoptive mother which took me in, warmed me, fed me, and—which is most important—did not seek to intrude into my soul."

Take Me to the River

The next day I went down to the Dnieper—as I mentioned earlier, I used to live near its banks. The older boys had a very effective way of teaching us younger ones to swim here: they would simply toss us into the water from a boat, and we would have to swim for our lives. One winter a friend and I were on the river when the ice cracked, and we went under. I have never forgotten how unbearably heavy my coat seemed; the white ice under which I was trapped suddenly seemed to turn pink. I suppose at that moment I must have started to slip away from life, but we were saved in the nick of time.

I always used to come down here to the river when I was feeling low, when I was hurt, when friends betrayed me, when my father died, when a girl I was in love with broke off with me.

I sat down on the bank and started tossing pebbles into the water. The blue waves of the Dnieper murmured their familiar refrain and the harsh cries of seagulls were just like they had been all those years ago . . . and life seemed to be nothing more than the short flight of the pebbles I cast into the river.

Such was my mood that day in Kiev. But I realized that I had to shake off the spirit of melancholy. I had only a few days left in Russia. When I returned to the U.S., I could reflect day and night. But for now, time was short, I had more contacts to make, and God had more adventures in store for me.

CHAPTER TWELVE

Last Days in Kiev

May God go with you, until
we meet again.
(From a Russian hymn)

August 19–23, 1988 . . .

My biggest disappointment, since leaving the Soviet Union over ten years ago, has been the separation from my family. Emigration brought freedom to my immediate family, but my extended family ties have suffered in the intervening years. One of the great joys of my 1988 tour was to see my relatives again after such a severe separation. When I emigrated, many of them were summoned to a "very important government organization" and forbidden to correspond with me. In fact, some of my friends received similar orders. To this day, I am convinced that this prohibition was thought up by someone of incredible stupidity. In fact, I can almost picture such a petty official. I can only hope that under Gorbachev he has been relegated to some other duty, nothing more weighty than the post of a bank manager.

I was blessed to see cousins, nephews, nieces, and aunts. I could not get my fill of gazing at their dear, familiar faces. Time had left its mark on them, but that was to be expected. My aunt lovingly fussed about, piling rissoles on to my plate, "Come on. Eat up. When you were little, my rissoles were your favorite dish!" This was not, as far as I could remember, true, but I nodded obediently.

My family told me about their lives and asked questions about ours. However, it quickly became very difficult and dull.

I knew that I should not feel like that, but I couldn't help it. Allow me to explain further.

As was to be expected, after the first hugs, kisses, and tears of welcome, the questions started to come thick and fast. At that point I came up against an insoluble dilemma. When I talked about life in the West, my relatives could not really understand me. They simply had no point of reference. Admittedly, over the past three years, there have been many chinks made in the Iron Curtain: Western radio stations are no longer jammed, an increasing number of Soviet citizens have been allowed to travel to the West, and the Russian press has started to print the truth much more frequently. Yet despite all this, after seventy years of distorted information about the West, it is hard for people—even psychologically impossible— to change overnight and begin to really understand.

For this reason, I could not but help feeling that much of what I was saying was simply not being assimilated by my listeners. The things I once had in common with them were no longer there. In the end I realized that this is not because of the years which have elapsed since I last saw them, but because I, as a former Soviet citizen, coming to the USSR on a visit, now had experienced life in two countries. As I talked, I unconsciously drew on this double experience, the experience of comparison. As for my friends and relatives, their experience was limited to life in the Soviet Union. Thus, the two sides, to use radio terminology, broadcast to each other on different frequencies. And for that reason, we did not really understand each other. Ultimately, we were left with the frustrating conclusion of not being able to "connect."

Such bittersweet personal experiences taught me, in such cases, to remain calm, avoid arguing, and try to keep peace with those I encountered on such terms. Naturally, there were matters of principle which could not be overlooked, which demanded a response or an explanation.

However, I do fondly recall that the people with whom I met and spoke responded much more openly to matters of a spiritual nature. I do not know why it was so, but I thank God for this oasis in the desert.

A Visit to the Past

After a day of family time together, we went to the cemetery. I bought a lot of flowers to place on the graves. Many of those who had been close to me and whom I had loved had died since I last set foot on Soviet soil.

I stood by the graves of my father, my uncles, and my friends. In Russia, it is a common practice to have photographs of the deceased on the headstones. I looked at the smiling faces of those who are no longer with us and thought that soon everything will pass by, and we all shall set forward on a long, unknown, and mysterious journey. Hinting at heaven, I said something of this to my relatives, and remarked that I had read somewhere that a child is born with its tiny fists clenched, as if to say: "Look! I will take the whole world into my hands!" Whereas we leave the world with our hands open—we take nothing with us, for we will need nothing in the place to which we go.

Finally, I asked my family whether I could pray for them all. And as I prayed, quite unexpectedly, I recalled the words of the old Hebrew poet Moshe ibn Zer, who wrote the following lines 900 years ago in Spain:

Let man remember and repeat,
That his path leads toward the grave,
And every day a little more advances,
Although he thinks that he stands still,
As one, who on a ship wind-driven,
Lies upon deck, eyes firmly closed.
No day is further than the one gone by,
No day is closer, than the one to come.

Irpen: Another Stop on the Trek

My next public appearance was in Irpen, a suburb of Kiev. This was a place I also remembered very well. It was here that there was a writers' "creative house." Gigantic pine trees arrow up toward the sky, their lofty tops reaching for the passing clouds, waving their green mane in their wake—once I knew many trails through these pines. It was here, in the silvery light of a sickle moon that we would congregate to talk about the meaning of life, joy, pain, and love. At that time life seemed understandable and endless. None of us thought that only one thing endows this fleeting moment with meaning and partially lifts the veil of its mystery. None of us, then, joined five ordinary letters—j, e, s, u, s—to form "Jesus."

It was unbearably hot in Irpen at the Christian Evangelical Church where I spoke. Not only are there no air conditioners in Russian churches, there are not even any fans. I was very conscious that this would be my last chance to speak in Russia, for in two days we would have to say farewell.

When I looked at the people who had gathered, I sensed on their part some kind of pure, childlike expectation of hearing something special; I felt an enormous wave of tenderness toward them. I talked about farewells: farewells at railway stations, farewells to our loved ones, farewells for a time and forever, and finally about the farewell of Christ.

Then I told them about the way a Russian Christian in Paris, the Orthodox nun Mother Maria, said farewell to life when she was sent to the Nazi concentration camp in Ravensbruck. There she gave up her life for a young Jewish woman who was holding an infant in her arms. Mother Maria went into the gas chambers with the name of Jesus Christ on her lips.

I also told them about the last moments of the German pastor Dietrich Bonhoeffer, who was hanged by the Nazis two weeks before the end of the war. Many Russians do not know that there was an underground evangelical church headed by this pastor in Hitler's time. They do not know that Bonhoeffer took part in Admiral Canaris' unsuccessful assassination plot against Hitler, and for this, was sentenced to death.

I read to them the account of the prison doctor, who saw Bonhoeffer in his last hours of life: "On 9 April 1945, between 5 and 6 o'clock in the morning, the prisoners—including Admiral Canaris and the Generals Oster and Sach—were brought out of their cells to hear the verdict. I saw Pastor Bonhoeffer on his knees in fervent prayer. The burning faith and unshakable hope in God, which were demonstrated so clearly by this amazing man's prayer, moved me to the depths of my soul. In fifty years of medical practice, I have never seen anyone give themselves so wholly into God's hands while facing imminent death."[1]

Bonhoeffer's amazing story is one with which I believed my Soviet audience could easily identify. I closed my talk by challenging my hearers to imitate Bonhoeffer's faith.

Then came the time for me to say good-bye to everyone. Those who have had occasion to be in Russian Baptist churches will know that when the faithful say farewell to someone, they do so by singing "God go with you, until we meet again" and wave white handkerchiefs.

A Disciple's No Better Than His Teacher

On the following day I managed to pay a quick visit to one of my schoolteachers, who had always tried hard to make me (as he put it) into a normal human being. He had aged greatly. I remember a lot of my teachers, but only a few with affection. This particular teacher taught me to love the Russian language and was delighted by my modest literary achievements.

When I was preparing to emigrate, he was quite upset. "It will be very easy for you to lose touch with the language over there," he kept repeating.

Yet now he harrumphed in a pleased sort of way, and even uttered some words of praise, "Good lad, everything you say on the radio is well-worded. I believe you've started to pay even more attention to the language than before. I give you top marks!"

I hugged him, gave him one of my few remaining Bibles and a cassette with my best known program on it, "Farewell, Cranes!" As we said our good-byes, he added, "The most important thing in life is to let nobody steal our life."

I embraced him again, and thought how big and strong he had seemed to me many years ago. Yet now, he too needed someone to support him, to say a kind word. And I thought once more of the wise words of Ecclesiastes 3:1: "To everything there is a season, and a time to every purpose under the heaven."

---

[1]Jacques Loew, *La Prière à L'Ecole des Grandes Priants,* ed. Foyard, Paris, 1975.

You Never Know Who Is Watching

On the last day I had an interesting encounter. While walking down the street I suddenly realized that I was under surveillance by four plainclothes KGB men. Three of them lounged near the hotel entrance, reading the same newspaper. The fourth one stood across the road, seemingly engrossed in studying his shoes. To their surprise—and my own!—I went striding over to them.

I challenged them, "You're not doing a very good job, are you? I could see at a glance that you're supposed to tail me!"

I thought their eyes would pop out of their heads. "OK," I continued, "I've got a proposition to put to you. Either you clear out of here right away, or I'll phone your bosses and tell them that I honestly think you're useless at your job. And that includes that 'professor' over there," I added, pointing at the man who stood across the street looking foolish.

After a few moments' thought, they decided that discretion was the better part of valor. You can't blame them—why should they risk trouble at work because of some weird Russian-speaking American? In twenty minutes' time there was no trace of them. I guess my point is that there are times when the KGB is not quite as frightening as it is painted.

Slow Train to Moscow

At last it was time to prepare for our trip home. My daughter and I left Kiev and returned to Moscow by train. An unexpectedly large number of people came to see us off: believers, friends, and relatives all gathered. There were even people whom I couldn't recall meeting before. There was the usual hustle and bustle of good-byes at the station. Flowers, exclamations, messages, and reminders blanketed us—in short, everything that is associated with the sad but lovely word "farewell."

"I don't know whether I'll ever see any of you again," I said to them, "but then—everything is possible. Yet I would like you all to know that I love you now more than ever before."

"So do I," said my daughter. I was very proud of her in that moment.

As the train pulled out the platform slid away, the figures of our friends grew smaller, and we could no longer hear their voices. Soon, all that remained were the shadows which faded into darkness.

We found ourselves in a carriage full of senior Soviet army officers. We must have been put in with them due to some bureaucratic error. The generals eyed us with unconcealed surprise. One of them, a classical stereotype of a general with a close-cropped brush of mousy hair, had clearly had a glass or two of cognac, so he ventured a question. "How did you get in here? Are you a military man?"

Quickly I replied, "In a manner of speaking, I suppose I am—an awkward soldier in Christ's army. Apart from that, I'm just an ordinary American citizen who speaks Russian."

The general shied away, and it seemed to me that the bristles on his head stood on end.

"What's the big deal?" I said, with feigned surprise. "Don't you know any ordinary Russians who speak English?"

"Not ordinary ones!" he barked, then he stamped his foot and disappeared into his compartment. However, a moment later he stuck his head out again, and added a waspish rider, "You don't look mentally ill, yet you mention Christ."

"Maybe it's those who *don't* mention Him who are mentally ill!" I snapped back irritably.

His steely eyes continued to stare at me for about another twenty seconds, and then he retreated, slamming the door.

The rest of the trip was uneventful. Russia slipped away past the windows. Aspens and birch trees seemed to run stumbling, like village girls, alongside the tracks. Their branches were like hands, extended in farewell. Some strange but somehow familiar lines came to mind:

Among your snows, before my very eyes,
I see a joyous carnival of birches.
I bow my head to you so low,
My country, always my first ball. . . .

Who wrote those lines? Heavens, it was me, back in the seventh grade, I think. I don't bow down to countries now, though—only to Him.

Reflections on My Generation

My generation, which came into the world in Stalin's times, still bears the wounds of the lies and psychological distortions to which we were subjected. All the generations of the Soviet regime are lost generations. But many in the first generation, that of our grandfathers, honestly believed that Communism would bring happiness and well-being to their country, at least, if not to the whole world. Our fathers, who came up against the terror and the prisons, taught themselves to close their eyes and continued to assert that Communism was the bright hope of the future for humanity. As for us—we were deceived from childhood by the totalitarian apparatus of lies, and spent part of our life under its anesthetic.

Then, in Khrushchev's times, we began to understand (as if we hadn't realized it for ourselves by then!) that all that had been was no more than a massive lie, a charade. Lies were cloaked in white and presented as truth, while truth was driven and imprisoned behind impenetrable walls. Cruelty was dubbed kindness, and children who informed on their parents were proclaimed heroes. The ungifted were hailed as masterminds, and geniuses were put to torture. The miserable were forced to declare that they could not be happier. And the ringmaster of this grotesque circus was a bowlegged, pockmarked mummer, a monster dressed up in the royal robes of the Father of the People. When we understood this, our hearts were torn asunder.

One part remained the same, and continued to cry out sincere oaths of loyalty to Stalin and the Party. The other half, disillusioned, lost faith in everything except the force of power, and became overshadowed by fear and thus largely inert, cynical, and suspicious. This fear is well illustrated in a poem by the Russian poet Lev Khalif:

What is your shell made of? I asked a tortoise.
And it replied: From all the fear I have lived through—
There is no surer shield than that.

As for those who came after us—they do not believe in much, but they do have at least a tiny grain of faith. Furthermore, they have a great advantage over my generation: they have no personal recollection of that terrible, numbing fear. And those who have no fear may one day come to believe in their dreams and, even more importantly, begin to take steps to realize them.

CHAPTER THIRTEEN

Glasnost-Perestroika: Open Door or Window Dressing?

What has *perestroika* given us? The
truth (Pravda), the whole truth, and
nothing but the truth.
(Joke about *glasnost*)

Since my return to the States, many people have asked me
two questions, time and time again. Is *glasnost* genuine, or is it
a well-conducted exercise in window dressing? And if the
person asking happens to be a believer, he will also add, Has
the situation of Christians changed in the USSR?

These two questions are intimately connected, so I will give
a combined answer. *Glasnost* is a fact. It does not yet extend
equally to the entire country, but it is a real force to contend
with nonetheless.

The Seeds of Change

Glasnost—which was initiated from the top, not the grass-
roots—is gradually penetrating all spheres of life in the Soviet
Union. It does so slowly, painfully, frequently inflicting heavy
wounds. But it has also touched the most oppressed sphere of
life—religion. The Soviet power apparatus reacts very quickly
to orders from the leadership if these orders do not threaten
its own positions of power. In recent times, the prevailing
opinion is that relaxations concerning religion do not pose any
such threat. The change in attitude began very cautiously,
with lyrical articles in the press about the moral values of the
nation and hints that there are positive aspects to Christianity.
A number of well-known "hack" writers quickly seized the

opportunity to present themselves in a "heroic" light by calling for publication of the Bible and the opening of churches.

It must be noted that to become a hero—a hero of *perestroika*—is much safer nowadays than at any other time under the Communist regime. One may make a few enemies, but it is patently obvious that manifestations of heroism today are no longer followed automatically by loss of life. That is why there are now veritable legions of heroes who proclaim loudly, anywhere and everywhere, that they would lay down their lives to ensure the success of *perestroika*. They see themselves as latter-day Parisian communards, manning the barricades against the conservative opposition. Yet it's an interesting fact that nobody has ever actually seen this opposition—for all that so much is said about it and so many efforts are pitted against it.

There appears to be an invisible opposition. Like an infection, nobody can see it but everyone fights it. Of course, there is an opposition. However, it is not some organized force, or a group of people united by a single aim—its the enormous, sprawling, glutted bureaucratic apparatus of parasites, who cling with bulldog tenacity to their powers and privileges. Yet for all its dullness and lack of initiative, the apparatus is extremely adept at protecting itself and its own interests. And this ability has come to the fore in connection with the new reforms. In the early days of *perestroika*, the bureaucracy did not grasp the situation at once, and its reaction was sharply negative to the new initiatives from the top. Drawing on past experience, the bureaucrats decided that this was just a lot of empty talk accompanying the ascension of a new General Secretary of the Party to the imperial throne. But as soon as it became clear that it was not just words, the apparatus did its faultless chameleon trick and changed its colors to those of enthusiastic supporters of *glasnost* and *perestroika*. The result is that at first Gorbachev and his small group of daring supporters at least knew who was on their side, and who wasn't. Now, however, all enemies wear the guise of friends. So the reformers are up against a deeply concealed secret opponent—an invisible apparatus.

Christ and Culture

Let us return, however, to the careful press campaign for restoration of national ethical and religious values. Soviet citizens, especially low and middle-level bureaucrats, excel in reading between the lines; they understood at once that the "courage" of journalists and writers had been approved at the highest levels.

In other words, Soviet mentality interprets this as a kind of unvoiced directive to be brave too. And they reacted accordingly: active persecution of believers fell sharply (not everywhere, but in many places), and permission was given here and there for the opening of churches. And then there was the sensational release of a large number of believers, formerly imprisoned for their religious activities. In several cities there were even attempts at some sort of dialogue between believers and atheists, and some of these discussions were shown on television in a positive light. This was after countless pamphlets, films, and books in which believers had been uniformly depicted as ignorant fools and accused of such atrocities as blood-sacrifice of children. After such endless vile slanders and mudslinging, this turnabout seemed positively miraculous. But the most important thing is that the winds of *glasnost* lifted the veil off something that had been painstakingly concealed by the authorities: that there were tens of millions of passive Christians in the Soviet Union, as well as those millions who had been open and active even earlier.

It is a notable circumstance that these are people who came to faith under the Soviet regime. Does this not prove, beyond any doubt, the miracle that God remained in Russia always, that evangelization continued, in one way or another, despite everything? Certainly, a significant role was played by Christian broadcasts from the West and Christian literature, yet one must not underrate the indestructible nature of the roots of Christianity in Russia, the presence of Christ in the hearts of her people. No matter how hard He was driven here, no matter what efforts were made to combat Him, no matter how often He was recrucified, He remained. He was among those whom Dostoyevsky called "the belittled and the abused"; He anointed their hurts, so that they would be, as Isaiah said, healed by His wounds.

The fresh breath of *glasnost* has made it possible for people to be more open about their faith in Christ, speaking of Him and witnessing without fear of retribution. This is true for the present, anyway. As well as more active churches, there are now numerous groups all over the Soviet Union who see Christ as the only path to renewal for the people and the country as a whole. I agree with them for the most part, because I have always maintained that it is impossible to build a contented society without transforming humankind first.

There can be no *perestroika* without a preliminary renewal of spiritual consciousness. Perhaps it is possible to bring about a change in the country just by altering people's mental attitudes, making them more efficient, conscientious, and calculating. Then, surely, there would be plenty of good quality jeans for everyone. There would be refrigerators, cars, and as much sausage as one could eat. But that would be all. People would become accustomed to driving cars and to having sufficient food, but would eventually find themselves at an impasse—because there would be no further *interests*. If it is not only the mind, but the soul which undergoes transformation, and is filled with spiritual freedom, love, forgiveness, and compassion—then Christ is essential. A new, harmonious Man will appear only when mind and soul are transformed simultaneously. And following the new Man will come a new society.

A Religious Revolution

Religious intellectuals talk about a phenomenon which will sound strange to Western ears, but which is a typical contemporary issue in Russia. How can I best formulate it? Perhaps the closest definition is a seemingly contradictory term: believing atheists. To put it simply, these people are atheists who talk about love and virtue because it is fashionable to do so, but without the underlying foundation of Christ. Such people find it very easy to change, from good to evil, from love to hate. There are and always have been plenty of people like that the world over, particularly in Russia. Many Russian writers have written about this, but it was Dostoyevsky—that great Russian writer of Polish extraction, exceptional Christian seer and genius and oddity in one, who expressed it better than anyone else—writing as he did with pain, concern, and unique vividness.

What else can be seen on the surface of that unexpected spiritual iceberg? Well, it should be remembered that Soviet citizens are unaccustomed to freedom, and therefore unaccustomed to the inevitable appearance of burgeoning, ugly weeds and thorns alongside the tender new shoots of liberty. Therefore we have seen the emergence of organizations which masquerade under the guise of Christianity, but in reality pursue only narrowly chauvinistic, distorted nationalist aims. The most prominent of these is the *Pamyat* (Memory) Society. Ostensibly, the group is campaigning against the destruction of Christian churches, but it is quite clear that their real agenda is to criticize all the nations of Russia apart from the Russians themselves, even though there are 135 non-Russian nations in the Soviet Union. It is said that *Pamyat* has some 30,000 members. Their slogans and idiotic allegations would be comical if it were not for the lessons of the past.

Incidentally, the Soviet authorities now acknowledge openly that there are neo-Nazi groups in the USSR. In the Central Asian republics there has been an emergence of "Muslim Renaissance" groups, whose statements echo those of the late Ayatollah Khomeini. Such phenomena are an inevitable byproduct of political freedoms in any country.

The authorities are not engaging in any mass persecutions of Christians at the moment. Naturally, this is not just because a few writers have spoken favorably of Christ, nor because Gorbachev feels any special sympathy for religious believers. We must not forget that the regime in Russia has not changed—not yet. The Soviet government is still in power; only the leadership has changed. It is much more flexible and contemporary, and, in the eyes of the West, appealing.

This latter tendency is understandable. Gorbachev is a far cry from such former leaders as Khrushchev, a ridiculous charlatan who could not tell the difference between the Rus-

sian words for "abstract art" and "homosexuality," and behaved like an unmannered swine in the United Nations. Brezh-
nev was no better, mumbling primitive platitudes, and wholly
disinterested in anything but collecting medals and motor cars,
pressing unwelcome, sloppy kisses on Party colleagues, and
visiting foreign dignitaries and film actresses. Compared to
them, Gorbachev seems exceptionally elegant, businesslike,
and witty. So I repeat, all that has changed is the leadership,
not the system, and its declared aim of seventy years ago still
stands—*the eradication of God*. For according to the bedrock
laws of Marxism-Leninism, the people under its rule should
not believe in anything other than its ideology. Thus, if the
basic concepts of the authorities have not changed, and they
continue to pursue their aim to eradicate God, then the only
thing that has changed is the form of the struggle against
religion, and the current concessions are only a pragmatic maneuver to employ Christians for the furtherance of the state's
economic and other interests. The rationale is that since
Christianity has proved indestructible, it must be brought to
heel by other, more up-to-date methods. (The older, tamed
generations of believers are considered to be of no account.)

What the Future Holds
I think that there are two future alternatives for what is occur-
ring in Russia at the moment. The first is that the "old model"
government machine is undergoing repairs and reorganization,
in which case everything that I have said above concerning the
attitude of the authorities to Christians follows logically.

The second alternative is that there is a historic change of
regime underway, where the new regime, with a genuine
change toward believers, can shed the aim of eliminating religious belief. If that is the case, then we are witnessing the
death throes of the Russian version of Marxism. I think we are
standing too close to the events of the present to discern with
certainty, which alternative is the true one, whether what we
are seeing is a revamping of the old, or the emergence of the
new.

I recall reading an interview given in 1895 to the *Chicago*

Tribune by the man whose ideas split the world in two, Karl Marx. In that interview he stated that "with the development of socialism, religion disappears." If that is the case, I do not think Marx could take umbrage if I were to suggest that if Soviet socialism has been developing for seventy years and religion has not disappeared, then either it is not socialism, or Marx was wrong yet again in his predictions.

At present, it is possible to assume that the system is changing, and its tenet that "God must be destroyed" is being replaced by another, "one must live with God." This may raise a few eyebrows and skeptical smiles, but I do not exclude the possibility that circumstances can change. After all, nothing is permanent in world history. As for believers—it is even easier for them to expect changes, for they know that with God, everything is possible. After all, just a few years ago it would have seemed incredible to predict all prisoners of conscience would be released from prisons and camps, or that Soviet newspapers would expose the crimes of high-ranking Party leaders. Anyone prophesying that would have been regarded as mad. There is a sour Russian joke that ten years ago Gorbachev would have been sentenced to death for some of the things he has said. Nobody can say how long the current situation will last, but for today—it is there.

Yet, whatever the outcome, millions of people in Russia have turned their eyes to God despite the difficulties and instabilities of their daily lives. Surely this is another manifestation of the hand of the Lord. I often think that God chose Russia as a test site to demonstrate to the rest of mankind the results of even great countries turning away from the Creator. What happened to Russia is a matter of record. I cannot guess why God permitted this experiment. Was it to be an object lesson? Only He knows.

In any case, Russia remains the exposed nerve of humanity. She lives, after 1,000 years of Christianity and 70 years of compulsory atheism. The soul of Russia is cleft in twain, and it remains the battleground between Christ and Satan. Every day, her people must choose whom to crucify and whom to spare. Ultimately, her fate will be decided by her final choice of either the emperor, or the "King of kings."

Not only Russia's fate hinges on this vital choice, but, in many ways, the fate of the whole of mankind. So I call on everyone to add their voices to my unworthy prayer, and ask Christ not to turn away His face from my first love—Russia— in this crucial time of desperation, pain, and hope.

EPILOGUE

Where can man's soul fly for rest?
To the hearth.
(from Russian folklore)

When I returned home, the friendly houses of little Glen Ellyn, Illinois looked like something out of a fairy tale. I felt warm and comfortable inside, almost a bit intoxicated. In the evening I watched people mowing their lawns and working on their homes. I inhaled the smell of hamburgers and Italian sausages from backyard barbecues. The leaves on the trees murmured soothingly, dogs barked lazily, and I could hear the excited cries of boys playing baseball.

Finally, I realized the reason for my contentment—*I had come home.* I had paid a visit to my slightly aged first love and then returned to my family, where I am respected and loved. At home nobody tries to pry into my inner thoughts. I can write about anything I like, including my "first love," without fear of a fateful hammering on my door in the middle of the night. On top of that it was here, in America, that I really came to Christ. That means that this country is the country of my first—and, I trust, eternal—love, however banal that might sound.

I remember how, once, a New York friend of ours, an art historian, questioned me eagerly about a trip I had made to Spain, Italy, and France, about the Salvador Dalí museum, other artists, and the Venetian school of painting. She was absolutely astounded when I said that I had found myself missing America while I was in Europe. I dare say if I were to tell her I missed America when I was in Russia, she would think that I was either joking or had gone completely out of my mind.

And yet . . . in September, when the forests of the Midwest don their yellowish-green autumn hues above cerulean lakes, I took my youngest son to one of the many local parks. When it grew dark, we saw children and adults heading for the lake with torches. Apparently some of the locals were staging a traditional enactment of an Indian ritual. The participants were dressed up in leather jackets and moccasins, with feathers in their hair. A boy was beating on a large drum. Someone lit a campfire beside a huge tepee, and hundreds of tiny flames snaked upwards toward the night sky. At the same time, canoes came drifting up on the waters, illuminated by burning torches.

The master of ceremonies recited some kind of incantation which was obviously known to all, because they chorused responses at the appropriate times. Then he led the singing of haunting, unusual songs, and everyone joined in, young and old. My son and I were the only ones who remained silent, because all this was new to us. As for the others—they had known it from childhood, from kindergarten through to college. Of course, I could always try to learn this too, but they would never really be my songs, my jokes, or my campfire smoke.

Such are the thoughts that came into my mind, while my son's dark eyes watched the Indians with concentration, and his lips moved in an effort to join everyone else in song. This was his land. I thought, he could learn the American rituals as an American. I, on the other hand, would always have a foot in another land—in fact, on another planet—my red one.

Well, my son, there is a time for everything under heaven. Soon you too will sing with the others, learn the correct responses, understand every joke, and the smoke from the campfire will be *your* smoke.

APPENDIX

The following is the text of a speech delivered by Konstantin Kharchev, Chairman of the Council for Religious Affairs in Russia, in March 1988.[1] The speech was secretly recorded. Presented here is a translated transcript of that recording, with only minor revisions. It is included here to demonstrate the Soviet government's attitude toward religion. Unfortunately, due to technical problems, the speech comes to an abrupt ending and is incomplete. However, the spirit of the address nonetheless is clearly communicated.

Statistics from the 1950s yielded some very unexpected results: that 70 percent of the population of the USSR—that is, 115 million people—are religious believers, although the official claim was that only 20 percent of the population were religious. Church leaders claim the figure of 70 percent, and I am inclined to believe them in this instance. Of these 115 million, 30 million are Orthodox Christians.

Let us consider the historical facts: confrontation between the Soviet authorities and the Russian Orthodox Church, which arose because the adherents of the church resisted

[1]Reliable sources report that Kharchev was removed from his post in April 1989.

Soviet power by force of arms, ceased in 1924 with the recognition of the new regime by Patriarch Tikhon. The years of collectivization and struggle against the "kulaks" were years of repression for the Russian Orthodox Church too because it was imperative to break down the ideology of the peasantry. In the 1930s, especially in 1937–38, church people were repressed on par with Party members.

The exigencies of the war years brought about a resurgence of the church. For ideological reasons, the Germans opened thousands of new churches in the territories they occupied. [In response to a query from the audience: "Hitler's *Mein Kampf* speaks of the need to destroy religion and replace it by occult sciences."]

However, Hitler was fully aware of the political importance of religious matters. Concessions had to be made to the church. During the war years, 2,500 churches were opened. The 1950s, in their turn, saw a burgeoning of religiosity. Khrushchev anticipated a speedy attainment of Communism; therefore, an end had to be put to the church as quickly as possible. From 1961–64 saw the closure of 10,000 out of 20,000 existing churches. Up to 150 churches a day were closed.

Some 1,300 churches were closed in the 1965–85 period. At present, there are 6,800 working churches. There are 57 functioning churches in Moscow and, although this number is clearly insufficient to meet the needs of the Muscovites, we have not received a single request from them for the opening of any new churches. At the moment there are some 1,000 "trouble spots" in the USSR, where citizens are demanding the opening of churches and registration of communities. The current trend of Party policy is that it is essential to review the 1929 legislation on religious cults and implement Lenin's decree on the separation of church and state. Incidentally, the 1929 legislation is a blatant contradiction of the Lenin decree. I disagree with some of the provisions of the decree, for instance—the denial of juridical status to the church.

At this time, there is no noticeable decrease in religiosity in the USSR. One million religious funeral services are conducted every year. In other words, 20–30 percent of all deceased receive church burial. In my opinion, funeral services are the most accurate indicator of religiosity, for during his lifetime, the deceased would have lied in order to safeguard his job. Thirty percent of infants are christened. It used to be the practice to demand passports at the christening, and this enabled Party workers to locate citizens who had been christened by reference to passport details, and to take administrative measures against believers. This practice of demanding passports at the church is not even dictated by the 1929 legislation. And in any case, as the church is, by law, separated from the state, no church document is valid in government bodies, just as no civil document—such as ID, passport, and suchlike—is valid within the church. On our initiative, the demand that passports be produced in church has been rescinded. Strangely enough, the most strenuous opponents of the rescinding of this "unwritten law" turned out to be the clergy. The reason, however, is quite simple: the fee for an official christening is 6.5 rubles, whereas for a clandestine ceremony, the priest stood to earn up to 100 rubles at a time.

We, the Party, have fallen into the trap of our own anti-church policy of prohibitions and persecutions; we drove a wedge between the priest and believers, yet this did not increase the believers' trust in local government bodies, and the Party and the state are increasingly losing control over believers. Moreover, as a direct result, we have the emergence of "unspiritual believers"—that is, those who fulfill the rituals but are indifferent to everything—and most importantly, indifferent to Communism. So what is more profitable for the Party—an unspiritual, or a sincerely believing person? It is harder to exercise control over the unspiritual one. This may sound paradoxical, but it is not, in fact, a contradiction. We are faced with an amazing phenomenon: despite all our efforts, the church has survived, and not only survived, but entered into a process of renewal. Therefore, we must ask ourselves—what is better for the Party—a believer in God, a complete nonbeliever in everything, or a believer in both God and Communism? I am convinced that the wisest choice is the lesser of the possible evils. Lenin taught that the Party must retain control over all aspects of citizens' lives, and as believers exist, and history has shown that religion is here to stay for a long time yet, it is easier for the Party to turn sincere believers in God into sincere believers in Communism too.

We are, therefore, faced with the task of raising a new type of priest; the choice and appointment of priests is a Party matter.

For this, comrades, we need to employ Party know-how. I urge you to establish, as soon as possible, a scientific workshop, if not an entire institute, devoted to the study of relations between church and Party, and socialism and religion. We shall supply you with all the necessary materials. But at the moment, we do not have such a research body. Thus, in the period of repression and then the period of stagnation, matters were allowed to slide on the assumption that religion would wither away of its own accord given certain conditions.

Our greatest success in controlling religion and suppressing religious initiatives has been achieved among the priests and bishops of the Russian Orthodox Church. At first this seemed a cause for congratulations, but now it carries the threat of unforeseen repercussions. Despite the fact that the activity of the Russian Orthodox Church is controlled and confined, and its undertakings give no cause for alarm—yet it should never be forgotten that even the most cowed and beaten dog's patience has its limits! We cannot help being concerned by the strengthening of other confessions: Catholics, who are still managing to keep their heads above the water, and there are rapidly growing sects, some 57 denominations making up 15,000 communities. In the past, we directed our energies at suppressing the Russian Orthodox Church and left the sects unchecked because we feared that they would go underground and we would lose all control over them. But Catholics, Protestants, Baptists, Evangelicals, Adventists, and many others have centers and headquarters outside the control of the Soviet government, and their rapid expansion can have unpredictable consequences.

The Party is interested in promoting a new type of Orthodox priest. At present, many of them have no bond with their parishioners, they come from different localities, and even may be of different nationalities. A priest like this will show up once a week in a car, serve the liturgy, and be off again without exhibiting any interest in local matters. This state of affairs may even suit the priest in question because it relieves him of bearing any responsibility for the parish, its finances, or such mundane concerns as repairs to the church building. Then there is the local plenipotentiary who, when issuing a license to a priest, will warn him: take your 350 rubles, and don't stick your nose into anything. As for what goes on in the parish—nobody really knows: neither the priest, nor the plenipotentiary, nor the Party. Yet that 70 percent of the population who are religious believers are not a trifle to be disregarded. You can't pretend they don't exist; it is essential to work with them and influence them. Then there is the question of church restoration and repairs—after all, 2,000 out of 6,800 churches are graded as architectural monuments. Would it not be better if they were to be maintained by those who serve in them?

And now, let us take a look at the matter of children's education. Whether we like it or not, we cannot tear believers' children away from them. Although it is forbidden for children to serve in church, and the Russian Orthodox Church observes this prohibition, there is no way in which we can control the influence exerted on children among other confessions. In Lithuania, 20,000 children receive catechism—clandestinely, of course. When such a child asks why he has to sit in a shuttered room and why he can't tell anyone that he is receiving religious instruction, adults will say to him: "Because the government is the force of the Antichrist, and doesn't want you to learn about the eternal truth of what is good." It is not hard to imagine what such a child's attitude will be to the state when he grows up.

I can understand your indignation. I too am opposed to the teaching of religious instruction in schools. But what can we do? In the Central Asian republics there are thousands of underground *medressehs* (seminaries), where the teaching is positively medieval, and the attitude toward the government and the "unfaithful" defies description. I raised the question of education on a higher governmental level, and what answer did I get? "What next? Sunday Schools after seventy years of Soviet government!" Don't misunderstand me—I am against Sunday Schools, but we've got to do something.

Another point in Lenin's decree is that the church is not a body in law. But if you look elsewhere in Lenin's writings you will read: "Every public organization enjoys juridical status." And if the church is not a public organization, then what is it? There has been church property in Jerusalem since Czar Alexander's times. We assert: "This is the property of the Soviet people—return it to us!" And the reply we receive is: "We would, but to whom does it belong specifically?" I repeat—I am not disputing the substance of the Lenin decree. I want to remind you of Lenin's conviction that politics begin when millions are concerned. The policy of the Party toward millions of believers must be conducted in a way that will ensure our maximum advantage.

Consider the slogan: "The church is separated from the state, and the state from the church." How is that to be interpreted? Separated, but to what degree? After all, a priest is a Soviet citizen too—he puts his vote for us into the ballot box regularly. Then look at all these various committees and funds: for peace, for culture, for children—in all of them you'll see these. [At this point, Kharchev gestured to indicate clerical headwear and long beards. Response from the audience is laughter.]

Incidentally, when they began to appear on television, I received numerous phone calls, from Party veterans, among others, protesting: "Why is this allowed? It's religious propaganda!"

I answered that I was not the one who put them there. It is imperative for us to change our style of thinking about the church and the clergy. If someone close to us becomes a priest, we should not treat this as something abnormal.

One may think that there is some kind of penetration going on by the church into state policy. But let us look at things rationally. Whether we like it or not, religion is entering into socialism, or, rather, not merely entering, but gliding in on smooth rails. Yet, as it is, for we who hold the power, I believe that it is within our capabilities to direct these rails in a direction profitable to our interests.

When we began to acquaint ourselves with the experience of Hungarian Communists, we were astounded by the presence of priests in their parliament. In answer to our protests, the Hungarians replied: "It is the function of parliament to represent all sections of society without exception." From my own experience, I can recall only one instance of a priest being elected to a regional council of workers' deputies, somewhere in the Baltic states, I think. By the way, he did a lot of good.

I am not for the unification of church and state. The most important task at the moment is to exercise effective control of the church through Party policy. Our Council for Religious Affairs consists of sixty people only, and we simply cannot cope with theoretical and practical questions.

Let us consider such an aspect of the law on the separation of church and state as the prohibition on charitable activity by the church. In Moscow—and in all large towns generally—there is a drastic shortage of junior personnel in hospitals, of ordinary nursing staff. In Moscow alone, the shortfall is 20,000. Representatives of the churches have applied to the authorities for permission to engage in charitable activity. So what should our response be, yes or no? Of course, we can let them empty bedpans, but then again, how will that reflect on the political and moral image of Communists, if a patient goes to his death thinking that the Soviet state is incapable of supplying someone to bring him a bedpan?

Another reason why we cannot afford to allow the church to engage in charitable work is that the Catholics will seize on it at once. Mother Teresa of Calcutta has already offered, so have Protestants, Baptists, Adventists. As for the Orthodox Church—at present it is in such a cornered position, that it simply lacks the financial resources for anything of that nature.

We are faced with numerous problems, comrades. We have become accustomed to thinking that there's nobody but old women in the churches, but if you go into a church nowadays you'll see hale and hearty people of our own age and lots of young people. Just look at the social profile of the seminaries: 70 percent of the students are from workers' and peasants' families.

ANSWERS TO QUESTIONS FROM THE AUDIENCE:

Q: What breaches of Soviet law are committed by local state officials and by the clergy?

A: The most frequent breaches by local state officials are stubborn refusals to open churches; they also frequently interfere in believers' private lives. Say there's a believer at some place of work. It's dangerous to penalize him financially, so moral pressure is applied instead. His name never appears on the commendations bulletin board, he gets no certificates of merit, his fellow workers don't wish him happy birthday, and so on. To the best of my knowledge, no state official has ever been prosecuted for breach of the religious legislation. Yet priests are punished at every turn.

Admittedly, a recent incident caused quite an uproar: a regional Party secretary had to be relieved of his post, yet he retained Party membership. But that was an event quite out of the ordinary. They decided to combat religion in one area in Ukraine, and what measures do you think they devised? Measures reminiscent of the 1930s: militiamen surrounded a church in a large village, brought up a truck, seized all the icons like veritable barbarians, loaded up and drove off. However, there must be divine providence after all [laughter in the audience] because the truck became bogged down in the middle of the main street, and wouldn't go either backward or forward. And these officials and militiamen could think of nothing better than to start putting icons into the mud under the wheels of the truck (right under the noses of the believers!) in an effort to get it moving again! Well, finally it moved out of the muck; the remaining icons were driven out into a field and burned.

After this incident, there was nothing to be done but to

remove the local first Party secretary from his post, also the deputy ideological officer and a few others. We made good all the damage in the church, but for how many years to come will youngsters who go to that church be told that here, on this spot, there used to be an icon of John the Baptist, which was burned by the godless Communists? If actions of this kind continue, what will be the feelings of the populace toward the Soviet government? Remember, comrades, we still have many towns where food is rationed.

Q: When will it be possible to obtain a Bible without any problems?

A: There are too few Bibles, too few. Over a period of seventy years, only 350,000 have been printed. Now, at the time of the Millennium, the Patriarchate is printing 100,000 copies. We shall receive 100,000 from Sweden, and we will allow the Baptists to import a further 100,000 from abroad. [Voice from the audience interjects: "Not enough!"]

Yes, I agree that it's not enough. I took the matter higher, and was told: "You want too much!" In practice, there is virtually no church publication. The *Journal of the Moscow Patriarchate* comes out in 30,000 copies; that's a drop in the ocean. Now we also have the *Courier of the Moscow Patriarchate* which, I should mention, is beautifully produced, but it is a purely promotional publication—counterpropaganda destined for distribution abroad.

Slavic Gospel Association is an evangelistic arm of Christ's church serving the peoples of the Soviet Union and Eastern Europe as a nonprofit interdenominational mission. SGA takes the Gospel to Russian-speaking people through a variety of ministries—the production of Bibles, other Christian literature, shortwave radio broadcasts, Christian audio, and video tapes. Slavic Gospel Association also provides training for pastors in the Soviet Union and a helping hand to refugees who have come to the West from the USSR or Eastern Europe. The mission actively encourages prayer support by Christians in the United States for the people of the Soviet Union. For more information, contact them at:

> Slavic Gospel Association
> P.O. Box 1122
> Wheaton, IL 60189
> (312) 690-8900